Rc

6

658.4
K499p

Prisoners
of Leadership

Manfred F. R. Kets de Vries

WILEY

John Wiley & Sons
New York • Chichester • Brisbane • Toronto • Singapore

my parents,
my children,
Elisabet and Florian

Reproduction or translation of any part of this work
beyond that permitted by Section 107 or 108 of the
1976 United States Copyright Act without the permission
of the copyright owner is unlawful. Requests for
permission or further information should be addressed to
the Permissions Department, John Wiley & Sons, Inc.

This publication is designed to provide accurate and
authoritative information in regard to the subject
matter covered. It is sold with the understanding that
the publisher is not engaged in rendering legal, accounting,
or other professional service. If legal advice or other
expert assistance is required, the services of a competent
professional person should be sought. *From a Declaration
of Principles jointly adopted by a Committee of the
American Bar Association and a Committee of Publishers.*

Library of Congress Cataloging-in-Publication Data:

Kets de Vries, Manfred F. R.
  Prisoners of leadership / by Manfred F. R. Kets de Vries.
    p. cm.
  Bibliography: p.
  ISBN: 0-471-50069-0
  1. Leadership.   2. Management.   I. Title.
HD57.7.K48 1989
658.4′092—dc19

88-28698
CIP

Printed in the United States of America

10 9 8 7 6 5 4 3 2 1

Preface

At a time of rapid transformations and rising expectations, concern has been increasing about international competition and our ability to meet the world challenge to our industrial and managerial edge. Such are the times when leaders seem to be in great demand; such are the times when leaders make the difference. We should not forget that leaders are those who are expected to create new visions and unleash and channel the untapped talent that exists at every level of an organization. Leaders are those who must prepare our institutions for the challenges of tomorrow. As catalysts for change they have to set this process in motion.

Looking back over this century, we can say that we have had more than our share of leaders—good ones and bad ones. As a student of leadership, I have been fortunate to live in this period of time. In my case, the study of leadership has not been a detached academic exercise. On the contrary, I have been able to follow the rise and fall of leaders—corporate and political—at close hand.

When as a student in Holland I read Plato's *Republic*, I was particularly fascinated with the section where he described the qualities needed for and training of the philosopher-king. Those who may have thought that interest in leadership and leadership training is a relatively recent phenomenon are in for a surprise. As early as 386 B.C., Plato

iii

initiated one of the first leadership training centers in the world, an institute he called the Academy. What he tried to accomplish was to create a new type of statesman, a person who would be able to withstand the unwieldy pressures of office. Plato seemed to be quite aware of the darker sides of leadership. He developed a draconian curriculum to prevent them from coming to the fore. How successful he was is another question. However, his one venture in applying his knowledge (and learning about leadership firsthand) by intervening in politics in Syracuse as the tutor of the tyrant Dionysius nearly cost him his head.

After my early encounter with Plato's ideas, my need to study leadership systematically got its real start at a seminar entitled "Psychoanalytic Psychology and Management Theory" given by Abraham Zaleznik at the Harvard Business School. After Plato, Freud's insights into human nature were a revelation to me as they opened up a whole new dimension.

Stimulated by the seminar, I struggled with the question of why some leaders mysteriously change after their ascension to power. What happens to them? How do certain leadership qualities that are originally an asset turn into a liability? What does it actually mean to be a leader? And why are some people more susceptible than others to what I came to call the F-dimension (failure factor)—that is, the combination of psychological pressures that are outside of direct awareness but unique to leadership. Orson Welles's statement that "I started at the top and worked my way down" is more than just a humorous remark; it rings the bell of truth. At the time, I didn't have much to say about this strange phenomenon, but that didn't mean I forgot about it.

PREFACE

In my work as a teacher, researcher, clinician, and consultant, I have been fortunate to meet a wide variety of people in leadership positions. To actually deal with them and not just read about them has been a great learning experience. In addition, having come back to Europe after a lengthy stay in North America, I was struck by the diversity in styles of leadership, a factor that became an additional stimulus and source of inspiration. Moreover, my training, which paradoxically combines a knowledge of the "dismal science" (economics) with the "impossible profession" (psychoanalysis), has proven to be very useful in acquiring greater insight into the leadership mystique.

In writing this book, I have taken many of my examples from my own practice, research, and consulting experience. At times, for purposes of illustration, I have also resorted to a more psychobiographical approach using public information. I systematically apply my clinical background in trying to make sense out of the leader's experience. I hope that by so doing I will further advance our understanding of this important topic.

Writing may be a lonely act, but it is not done in a vacuum. Many people helped me while the project was on its way. For this I am deeply grateful. First of all, I wish to express my debt to Abraham Zaleznik, the Matsushita Professor of Leadership at the Harvard Business School, mentor, colleague, and friend. In many ways, without really knowing it, he was instrumental in getting this project off the ground.

I would also like to express my gratitude to Maurice Dongier of McGill University's Department of Psychiatry. I have tried to emulate his capacity for reflection and ability to see the unusual, which inspired me in writing this book.

Moreover, I am beholden to the creative thinking of Harry Levinson, Henry Minzberg, and Edgar Schein.

I am particularly indebted to Danny Miller of McGill University and HEC, Montreal. I often think nostalgically about our collaborative efforts before a continent split us apart.

I thank the students who stimulated me by asking the unexpected question, as well as my patients and clients, who placed their trust in me and taught me many fascinating things. I gratefully acknowledge my debt to them all and thank them collectively.

My colleagues Michael and Linda Brimm, Paul Evans, André Laurent, Susan Schneider, and Martine Van den Poel at INSEAD; and Alain Noel and Laurent Lapierre of HEC, Montreal, made invaluable comments concerning sections of the book. The insights of my two former assistants, Robert Dick and Jane Petrie, who have now gone on to greater things, were very much appreciated. In addition, I am very grateful to Joyce and Lawrence Nadler not only for their various ideas for improvements, but also for the opportunity they gave me to test those ideas in practice. I would also like to express my deepest appreciation for the editorial help of Sophia Acland, Eliza Collins, and Christina Davis. Their suggested improvements in presentation have made for a more readable book.

I wish to acknowledge the financial help I have received from INSEAD's Department of Research under Director Charles Wyplosz, assisted by Diane Mitchell. Their logistic support has been invaluable in making this book possible.

The typing of the various drafts has been done with much enthusiasm by my secretary Catherine Petts, who stood by me patiently and uncomplainingly, typing and retyping the manuscript more times than I care to remember. Here I also want to thank Henriette Robilliard, for managing the process. Moreover, I want to express my gratitude to Sylvie Exposito, Pia Arquati, and Helene Schieder in helping me finish my final draft.

As always, I would like to acknowledge my debt to my agent, Doe Coover, in helping me to bring the project to fruition. In addition, my thanks go to my editor at Wiley, John Mahaney, for his confidence in the project, as well as his incisive comments.

Finally, I wish to thank my wife Elisabet for her judgment, insight, and support throughout my writing. She not only provided the climate necessary for the work on this book, but also gave most valuable editorial assistance.

MANFRED F. R. KETS DE VRIES

Paris, France
February 1989

Contents

1. The Internal Psychic Theater of the Leader   1

2. Uncovering the Operational Code:
   The Enigma of Leadership   11

3. The Mysterious Transformation:
   Leaders Who Can't Manage   29

4. The Spectrum of Personalities:
   Leaders and Followers   53

5. Personal Glory and Power:
   Leadership in a Narcissistic Age   89

6. Folie à Deux: Leaders Driving
   Their Followers Mad   115

7. The Dark Side of Entrepreneurship   137

8. The Succession Game   163

9. "I'd Follow That Man—Anywhere—
   Blindfolded": Effective Leadership   187

10. The Leader as Symbol   213

    Chapter Notes   223
    Index   243

1
The Internal Psychic Theater of the Leader

One is tempted to define man as a rational animal who always loses his temper when he is called upon to act in accordance with the dictates of his reason.

Oscar Wilde, *The Critic as Artist*

When Carlo De Benedetti took over as chairman of Olivetti, the company looked like a basket case. Burdened with an obsolete technology, laden with debt, losing money at the rate of ten million dollars a month, the once-successful typewriter company was seen by many business analysts as an organization whose days were numbered. De Benedetti's decision to put his money on the line and buy into the company led many to wonder what had gotten into him and even conclude that he had signed his own death warrant. But De Benedetti proved all the doomsday prophets wrong. Under his charismatic leadership the tottering company was turned around and made into one of the most profitable and dynamic concerns in the world. An important factor in the turnaround was that De Benedetti managed to gain the respect of the trade unions. Realizing how desperate the situation was, he opened the company's accounts to the union officials, explaining to them that the alternative to his draconian recommendations was bankruptcy. He laid off almost twenty thousand out of a work force of sixty-five thousand employees, and this included the replacement of most top managers.

3

Through total immersion in the problems of the company he convinced the managers who stayed on that they once again could be part of a winning team and, more than that, that they could become the vanguard in fighting the existing malaise in Italian industry.

Another factor in his success was that with the breakup of AT&T he saw an opportunity and succeeded in closing an imaginative business deal involving a marketing and technology sharing arrangement, thereby in a single stroke making Olivetti a major player in the office automation market.

A number of years later, when asked by *Newsweek* what contributed to his success, De Benedetti replied "the Israel Effect." By this he meant that after having invested some seventeen million dollars of his own money in the company, his back was against the sea and he could not withdraw. To use his own words, "I [had] to win, because I had put in my own money and wouldn't have been credible in my own profession." And the "Israel Effect" has worked, as the profits at Olivetti and his successful participation in many other new ventures have shown. The timing was right, as De Benedetti was at a turning point in his career after his dramatic departure as managing director of Fiat. Moreover, Italy was also ready for him, antibusiness attitudes having reached an all-time high with disastrous economic results. Because of his contribution to Italy's economic turnaround, De Benedetti has become an example of the best Italian industry has to offer, being voted in 1985 the country's manager of the year. He has graced the covers of many business periodicals and has been included in *Fortune*'s list of top European managers. And his meteoric rise in the business world seems to be continuing as his entrepreneurial activities increase daily. In doing all this, De Benedetti has challenged the predominance of Italy's industrial and financial establishment, redrawing the country's industrial map, and with his new ventures outside Italy has become recognized as one of the world's "super managers."

Like De Benedetti, many of today's most successful business leaders are household names; their particular qualities and charisma have made them famous far beyond the confines of boardroom or factory. Indeed, many people identify particular companies with the personality of the leader. Carlo De Benedetti is a good example of such a leader but others can easily be found: Soichiro Honda of the Honda Motor Company, Armand Hammer of Occidental Petroleum, and Lee Iacocca of Chrysler are some of the best known.

Smaller firms less often in the headlines similarly can be dramatically galvanized by an exceptional CEO. A good leader can inspire subordinates to do things beyond their normally accepted capabilities, can foster their enthusiasm for challenging new ventures, and can give them the confidence to make them succeed. Exceptional leaders seem to have a mysterious power over their subordinates; they somehow seem to woo their followers into deep loyalty and almost unquestioning compliance with their wishes.

The high standards and fierce loyalty that H. Ross Perot, the former president of Electronic Data Systems (EDS), inspired in his workers is a good case in point. In many business periodicals, journalists marveled at the extent to which Perot expected his "troops"—a very appropriate description given the almost paramilitary culture prevalent in his company—to share his sense of dedication, and the extent to which they actually did so, willingly. To make this happen, a considerable amount of time was devoted to indoctrinating new recruits in Perot's way of thinking. And Perot's sense of egalitarianism in running the company's affairs certainly helped in obtaining the degree of commitment he wanted. As the president of EDS, Perot never believed in such things as executive dining rooms, special parking facilities, or similar privileges. To him every employee was a full partner. Probably adding to this sense of loyalty among his employees was Perot's spirit of adventure. His failed mission in 1969 to send two hired Boeing 707s to North Vietnam to take Christmas gifts to American prisoners of war is only one example. His most remarkable feat, popularized by novelist Ken Follett in his best-seller *On Wings of Eagles* and later serialized by NBC-TV, was his successful attempt to organize a commando team from among his employees that rescued two of his managers from an Iranian jail during the chaotic revolutionary days of 1978.

Truly great leaders, however, are few and far between. Many people, when they reach the top of an organization, cannot cope with the pressures of leadership. Spectacular failures have occurred, like those of John DeLorean of DeLorean Motors, Bernard Cornfeld of Investment Overseas Services, and Ernest Saunders of Guinness. Less well-documented failures occur every day. Some people simply seem unable to hold a position of ultimate responsibility; others may not succeed in convincing their subordinates that their vision of the company's future is the right one; still others may let power go to their heads and indulge in grandiose schemes that are beyond the scope of their organization. And given the CEO's power over the organization's resources, the damage that may be done by those who cannot lead is immense. A number of spectacular bank failures like Franklin National Bank or Penn Square Bank are good illustrations.

What is it, then, that makes a leader great? What gives leaders their mysterious power over others? Why do some succeed where others don't? And why is it so difficult to be a good leader? What are the pressures that are brought to bear on leaders? Is some kind of *failure factor* (F-dimension) inherent in leadership? What can leaders do to avoid this F-dimension or at least prepare for it?

Studies of leadership—and there have been many of them—have offered conflicting answers to these questions. The F-dimension in particular has remained an unexplored domain. To find one's way in the leadership literature is actually like walking on quicksand: there is very little to hold on to. Competing theories abound and confusion reigns. What is most discouraging is that in many leadership studies the focus is on abstract theoretical conceptualizations, while the object of investigation, the leader, seems to be conspicuously absent. This has caused one political scientist to say that "all paths to the study of leadership end up swallowing their subject matter."

To add to the problems, many leadership theorists seem to come down at opposite ends of a spectrum. For example, one school of thought views the leader as a marionette, a person who has very little influence on organizational decision making and performance. These scholars put forth the argument that socioeconomic factors and not leadership are what really make the difference. This "population ecology" outlook shows similarities with the arguments of those theorists who view organizations as basically

7

resource-driven. Control over the resources in the environment is what determines the direction of the company; hence, this way of looking at organizational life sees leaders as little more than puppets. To use the words of the Nobel Prize winner Herbert Simon, the leader becomes "a bus driver whose passengers will leave him unless he takes them in the direction they wish to go."

In sharp contrast to this way of thinking, the "strategic choice" theorists take the position that such a thing as purposeful action exists in organizations; leaders can make a difference and affect organizational outcomes. In this case—unlike in the marionette theory—the leader turns into an enchanter, dazzling others into following his or her lead.

As with most things, the truth lies somewhere in between. Without question, leaders are influenced by events, but they can certainly also be catalysts of events. Leadership is not merely the outcome of various social forces. Leaders can make a difference by virtue of their actions or even lack of action at important moments in time. Unfortunately, even if we lean toward strategic choice theory while paying attention to the impact of environmental forces, this approach can also turn sterile in the end, since it looks at leadership, like many other theories do, only at a surface level.

This book is different, however: it pays attention not only to the surface structure of a leader's behavior but also to its deep structure. It doesn't just look at simple behavior; it attempts to go further than that. As Thoreau allegedly once said, "What is the use of going round the world to count cats in Zanzibar?" Mere counting is not good enough. It is probably more important to understand why the "cats" are doing what they are doing. One has to go beyond the surface level. The only way to understand leadership is to dig deep, to probe the *inner* world of the leader. In other words, the complex psychological forces that go to make up the leader's personality provide the real key to his or her behavior. Thus, core themes in a leader's "inner theater" cause him or her to choose certain courses of action, and these themes hold the key to success or failure as a leader. Similarly, the key to a leader's relationship with his or her followers is the psychological forces at play between them. Such forces exist at the intrapsychic, interpersonal, group, and organizational levels. By examining these forces, we can understand how leaders influence followers and vice versa. We can also see the ways in which leaders can become prisoners of their internal psychic theater so that their actions become self-defeating. This destructive side of leadership is what I call the F-dimension.

This book is for leaders, aspiring leaders, and all who have to deal with them. Probing the inner world of the leader, it looks at both successful and unsuccessful leadership, showing what the ingredients of the former are and how to deal with the forces that tend to the latter. Concepts such as charisma and entrepreneurship are discussed, and also the often vexing question of leadership succession— how and when to choose an effective new leader. Throughout the book, I use case illustrations from my consulting experience and from studies of leaders in action.

My main objective throughout is to help the reader look beyond what is directly observable when studying the phenomenon of leadership. I want the reader to understand that the leader's task is paradoxical: at one level the leader appeals to the rational capacities of the followers, while

9

at another his or her message is aimed directly at their unconscious. Moreover, leaders are masters in the use of disguise, seduction, and manipulation. These facts are partly responsible for their mystique but at the same time create an element of bewilderment in those trying to see the deeper reasons behind their actions. Given the critical role leaders play, however, we should make this leap and look beyond the obvious and superficial. We should also be alert to a leader's darker sides and be aware of the F-dimension, for, as Thomas Jefferson once put it, "Whenever a man has cast a longing eye on offices, a rottenness begins in his conduct."

2
Uncovering the Operational Code: The Enigma of Leadership

The term "charisma" will be applied to a certain quality of an individual's personality by virtue of which he is set apart from ordinary men and treated as endowed with supernatural, superhuman, or at least specifically exceptional powers or qualities. These are such as not accessible to the ordinary person, but are regarded as of divine origin or as exemplary, and on the basis of them the individual concerned is treated as a leader. In primitive circumstances this peculiar kind of deference is paid to prophets, to people with a reputation for therapeutic or legal wisdom, to leaders in the hunt, and heroes in war.

Max Weber, *The Theory of Social and Economic Organization*

Historians, political and social scientists, and the like have tried to explain the mystique of leadership from different angles. In most instances their attempts at explanation have not led to greater insight, although some exceptions exist. One avenue that showed some promise was the concept of charisma. Charisma has often been used to explain the mysterious, almost mystical bond between leader and led, an interface that can have both constructive and destructive outcomes.

The sociologist Max Weber popularized the concept of charisma. He distinguished it from two other forms of authority, although he admitted the possibility of some overlap. For Weber, charismatic individuals differ from others in that they have the capacity to personally inspire loyalty, which is quite distinct from the authority derived from office or status. However, Weber did not apply the term *charisma* only to the gift of grace; the connotation of the extraordinary stood central in his description. Weber named as charismatic all people with inspirational gifts, individuals who could impose themselves on their environment and stand out because of their exceptional insight,

13

courage, energy, decisiveness, or other qualities. People with these characteristics were to be found in all realms of life.

Weber also mentioned the revolutionary nature of charisma—how such forms of leadership seem to emerge particularly in periods of uncertainty and unpredictability, times when psychic, physical, economic, ethical, religious, or political distress exists. Stable, well-functioning societies seemed to have less of a need for the services of such individuals. There may be some truth to his observation. When asked to name charismatic political leaders, we immediately think of individuals such as Napoleon, Lenin, Ataturk, Roosevelt, Churchill, Sukarno, Nasser, Nkrumah, Ben-Gurion, Mao, Tito, and Castro, each of whom took on the role of helmsman to steer his country through a difficult period. The same can be said, albeit on a lesser scale, for corporate leadership. Prominent individuals such as Lee Iacocca of Chrysler, John Harvey-Jones of ICI, and Jan Carlzon of SAS are good cases in point; each of them had to steer his company through a critical period in its development.

Charismatic leadership in action appears to some extent to be a function of the need for order. Paradoxically enough, in providing "deliverance," truly charismatic leaders tend to be revolutionary in that they may enter into conflict with the established order. But charismatic leaders solve this dilemma by creating order out of disorder: they provide their followers with new systems of coherence, continuity, and justice. The above-mentioned political and corporate leaders seem to have been very skilled in channeling grievances and diverging interests and concerns into common goals; they provided a focus for others. To some

14

extent their actions gave new meaning to the lives of their followers. "Salvation" was offered in the form of safety or a new identity, on a national or a corporate scale.

Weber also mentioned that charisma "may involve a subjective or internal orientation born out of suffering, conflicts, or enthusiasm." Although he did not have the advantage of clinical insight to help him understand the deeper structures that influence behavior and action and to help him probe the origins of the mysterious bond between leader and led, he may have been aware that certain not necessarily conscious forces were at play. In fact, what is called charisma can be considered part of a more widespread phenomenon. Charismatic elements are actually present in *all* forms of leadership and have their source in the psychodynamics of leader-follower behavior and the psychology of groups and organizations. Even quite ordinary people who find themselves in a position of leadership cannot escape them.

Unfortunately, in introducing and popularizing the concept of charisma, Weber did not really solve the mystery of the strange bond between leader and led. His analysis remained largely at a descriptive level, with the term *charisma* something of an afterthought. In spite of all his insight, charisma remained something he could not explain and so he glossed it over, relying instead on his other categories to explain authority relations.

Other students of charisma have not fared much better. Like Weber, they have not really been able to explain the nature of the psychological exchange between leader and led and the psychodynamic processes that come to the fore. Why some leaders fail and others do not and why such a thing as an F-dimension exists in leadership remain a

15

mystery. A deeper level of analysis is required to explain this enigmatic interface.

PRIVATE VICES, PUBLIC VIRTUES

For leaders to be effective, their own concerns must have some kind of congruence with those of society. Leaders gain conviction, power, and charisma by their ability to articulate the underlying issues of a society at a given time. In trying to solve their personal struggles, they manage to project these struggles onto their involvement in and solution of the problems of society at large. A leader's vision becomes the concern of all. According to the psychoanalyst and student of human development Erik Erikson, who uses such dramatic examples as Martin Luther and Mahatma Gandhi, such leaders lift individual problems to the level of universal ones, trying to solve for everyone what they originally could not solve for themselves. Internal, private dialogues are transformed into external public concerns.

How does this transformation take place? How does one's internal theater become externalized? How can we identify specific themes that characterize a leader's behavior? How can we make sense out of it? Unfortunately, there are no easy answers to these questions. It is usually hard to identify internalized, habitual rules of conduct in an individual, to find what has sometimes been called the operational code, and to discover what makes him or her tick. To understand leadership and followership, however, it is important to identify an individual's operational code or "core conflictual relationship themes"—that is, the consistencies in patterns of relationship. It is essential to find the constantly repeated patterns in a leader's life, given the importance of leadership to society. The system of underlying reactions of a leader is the key to understanding his or her wishes, needs, intentions, and ways of acting. An individual's style of leadership is very much determined by these core conflictual relationship themes. Moreover, if we identify the themes, more can be said about the leader's vulnerability to the F-dimension.

Let us take a business illustration. Throughout his career, the first Henry Ford was preoccupied with ameliorating the life of the farmer. Quite in contrast to more "normal" business practices, Ford allowed tractor production to be carried out at a loss. To everyone's surprise, when one of his senior executives told him about this, Ford responded by saying, "That's about the best information I've had; I'm glad of it. If we can give the farmer $55 with every tractor that's just what I want."

Conventional rationality does not seem to apply here. But with an understanding of Ford's core conflictual relationship themes, this statement may make some sense. If we look at other stressful incidents in his life we notice that the well-being of the farmer remained a constant preoccupation. For example, when Ford arrived in Oslo with his peace ship (his idea to stop the First World War), to the surprise of all journalists present he didn't talk about the prospects for peace, which, after all, was the supposed purpose of the journey. Instead, he again spoke about his tractor, which would take the drudgery out of farming. When pressured by the opposing attorney during a libel suit against the *Chicago Tribune*, Ford began inexplicably and to the great bewilderment of the audience to talk once again about tractor production.

For Ford, the Model T was the farmer's car, and by that right untouchable; it was produced without a single change for nineteen years. It was affordable and durable, lightening the farmer's burden and breaking his isolation and the monotony of his work.

All these otherwise strange incidents and irrational patterns of behavior can be seen as ways in which Ford's core conflictual relationship themes were externalized.

One way of interpreting his preoccupation with the exploited American farmer is to view it as Ford's way of overcoming his ambivalence about his dealings with his father, who was a farmer himself. This ambivalence may have been intensified by the death of Ford's mother in childbirth, an event for which he may have blamed his father. Apart from the reality component in all of this, we should keep in mind the possibility of what we call displacement activity: suddenly, what may have been the occasional hostile thought toward mother has become painful reality through her death. Defending oneself against feelings of guilt by making father the culprit becomes an obvious answer. These psychological contortions may, however, have left Ford with a legacy of anger about abandonment and at the same time guilt about his anger and imagined responsibility in the matter. He became the "bad son" even more when, as a young adult, he "abandoned" his father by leaving the farm to pursue his mechanical bent. One could speculate that his preoccupation with the Model T—the car that would take drudgery away from farming—or his need to produce tractors below cost were ways of expiating his feelings of guilt vis-à-vis his father. By externalizing his private conflicts and single-mindedly applying his concerns to a societal problem of the time, Ford was able to contribute to the transformation of America.

Ford's operational code became his formula for success —his notion of a cheap car for the masses and his introduction of the assembly line derive from it. But his operational code also led to his downfall because it transformed him over time into an irrational and rigid leader unable to change his initial formula or tackle other public problems successfully. That is when the F-dimension comes into the picture. We should keep in mind here that past relationships, especially with parental figures, become the matrix on which present relationships are built.

To give another, more recent example, let us look at Richard Branson, the unorthodox millionaire chairman of Virgin. His business empire includes such ventures as records, videos (for example, of Culture Club and the Sex Pistols), the Virgin Atlantic airline, film production, satellite communications, book publishing, and a chain of retail stores. The core themes in his internal theater most likely have something to do with being an explorer and "doing your own thing," remaining independent and being daring —that is, controlling your own destiny. We can speculate that these characteristics were instilled by a mother who was independent and daring in her own right. Her career (she was both a dancer and an air stewardess on the first scheduled air service over the Andes) is indicative of her own preoccupation.

We can assume that Branson's operational code was reinforced by a father forced into a career as a barrister by his own father. The middle Branson's natural reaction may have been to encourage his son to make his own

19

choices. The career of his grandfather, Sir George Branson, a high court judge, must have made quite an impact on the fantasy life of young Richard. His visits as a boy to the Chamber of Horrors in Madame Tussaud's waxworks, where some graphic displays of murderers hanged by his grandfather could be seen, may have nourished a wish in him to become as successful and powerful.

As an adult Branson certainly has been doing his own thing, having turned into one of the better-known public personae in England. He is the darling of Margaret Thatcher, the kind of person who will help her revitalize England. Branson is also the favorite of a new generation of business people, having gone "from the rock market to the stock market," the epitome of the modern dream of success. His head office on a houseboat is legendary, and accounts of his daring escapades such as Atlantic crossings by speedboat or hot air balloon have been broadcast around the world. He has become a prime example of the alternative capitalist.

His latest, more socially concerned ventures include the UK 2000 campaign, an employment project designed to enhance the environment, and the establishment of a health foundation to fight AIDS. And given the nature of his core conflictual relationship themes and their consequences for action, we can expect that more is to come. Branson will continue to be an "explorer" in the business domain.

The extent to which private crises influence public events was clearly articulated by the political scientist Harold Lasswell in his seminal work *Psychopathology and Politics*. According to Lasswell, the distinctive mark of *homo politicus* is the displacement of private motives onto public objects and, at the same time, the rationalization of these motives in terms of the public interest. Intrapsychic conflicts are acted out on the public stage. The effectiveness of this process of externalization depends, however, on the leader's ability to recognize the preoccupations emerging in society and make them meaningful. Speeches, ceremonials, and rituals are some of the vehicles by which the needs to be specified become externalized. To use the words of Marshall McLuhan, the medium becomes the message. In the sphere of business these rituals are connected to such events as special conferences, annual meetings, sales conferences, and even Christmas parties. It will come as no surprise that both Henry Ford and Richard Branson have been masters of the media.

The Mary Kay Cosmetics annual meeting is a particularly good example of a very successful business ceremonial where a private crisis is repeatedly externalized. The activity is used to foster identification with Mary Kay's "heroic" climb to fame: how, when deserted by her husband, she had to take care of her children and herself and thus ended up creating her company. During these meetings, staged like a Miss America pageant with lavish ceremony and a large, cheering audience present, bee-shaped jewelry (Mary Kay's personal symbol), fur coats, and pink Cadillacs are given to those saleswomen who have reached high sales quotas. In turn they tell how *they* have attained success, praising the founder for the opportunities she has given them. The Mary Kay rags-to-riches story surely hits a sensitive chord in the audience, since many of the women may have found themselves (or are afraid of finding themselves) in a position similar to that of Mary Kay (being deserted by a husband).

THE IMPORTANCE OF PROJECTION

An important factor in the relationship between leader and led that also contributes to charisma is the process of projection, the psychological mechanism of transferring or assigning to another an idea or impulse that really belongs to oneself. Leaders are prime targets for reflecting the wishes of their followers.

Jerzy Kosinski, in his novel *Being There* (later made into a film starring Peter Sellers), created a caricature of this process. The hero of the novel, Chance, a totally illiterate, mentally retarded individual, eventually finds himself chosen to run for high office. His vacuous remarks about gardening (the only topic with which he has some familiarity) are reinterpreted by all and sundry as highly incisive. Throughout the novel we can see how Chance's statements of ignorance on various topics become transformed by the receivers, who turn them into reiterations of their own desires. The people around Chance react only to what they want to see or hear.

Projective processes seem to play a major role in myth-making and symbolic action. Propelled by the complexity and ambiguity of the events around us, we choose leaders to make order out of chaos. Leaders become the ideal targets for assumption of responsibility for otherwise inexplicable phenomena. Desirable and undesirable ideas and perceptions are cast upon another. Good examples of these mechanisms at work are hero worship and scapegoating.

Given the existence of such processes, it seems that even if no one with leadership abilities were available we would have to invent such a person. We need someone to look up to or to blame. The mere presence of individuals willing to take on the leadership role facilitates the organization of experience and in so doing helps us acquire a sense of control over our environment, even if this is only an illusion. To illustrate the structuring experience leaders provide, consider the comments I once overheard from a senior executive in a furniture company: "Our president . . . what can I say? He is incredible. I have now been working with him for over three years, and he never ceases to amaze me. I don't know how he does it. Take his capacity for work. No matter what kind of pressure we are under, he seems to keep on top of things. Without him, we would never have done as well as we did.

"I still remember the day he hired me. The moment I met him, I knew we would hit it off. He taught me all that I know about this business. And still, I'm a long way from matching him. I would be lost without him. Working for him is the greatest experience I've ever gotten in life."

Through the projective process, leaders become the recipients ("containers") of other people's ideals, wishes, desires, and fantasies. Mystical, charismatic qualities are attributed to them, whether they possess them or not. And in accepting this role they may turn into master illusionists, keeping the fantasies they have provoked alive and conjuring up images of hope and salvation that may replace reality. Such projective mechanisms tend to appear particularly in times of distress. Crisis situations make for a sense of helplessness and may give rise to forms of collective regression.

Crisis situations, however, can also be seen as opportunities, since these are the times when core conflictual relationship themes come sharply into focus; these are the

23

times when we can learn more about the leader's susceptibility to the F-dimension. What we tend to observe when leaders and followers regress is how they may revert to more primitive patterns of behavior. Such incidents become a demonstration of how easily very archaic psychological processes can emerge and affect action. Freud, probably influenced by the events of World War I, had a good sense of what can happen when people get together in groups in this way: "All their individual inhibitions fall away and all the cruel, brutal and destructive instincts, which lie dormant in individuals as relics of a more primitive epoch, are stirred up to find gratification." Hitler's "final solution" for the Jews and the mass suicide that occurred at Jonestown under the Reverend Jim Jones are very dramatic examples of this phenomenon. Corporate life, however, is also rife with examples of regressive behavior. The Boesky affair and its aftermath on Wall Street is only one case in point.

The key question becomes why followers would go along with such practices. Why do they allow themselves to be drawn into the private neuroses of a leader? Why would they join in making the F-dimension operational? According to Freud, the appeal of leaders is that at a more symbolic unconscious level they represent the return of the primal father with whom, like the father of early childhood, it is easy to identify. Not only do followers identify with the leader but also with each other, thereby laying a base for group cohesion. Reinforcing the group process is the illusion that the leader disperses favors and imposes deprivations on an egalitarian basis. The followers' hopes and exaggerated wishes are projected onto the leader. With their own internal demands and prohibitions dissipated (transferred to the leader), they experience a sense of relief and a feeling of community. The followers no longer feel harassed by prohibitions; they have no more pangs of conscience. The leader turns into the conscience of the group. Moreover, the leader, as the tangible representation of the followers' lofty ideals, creates in the followers a temporary state of euphoria. The suspension of the tension between one's perception of oneself and the image of what one would like to be contributes to this euphoric state.

This kind of abdication of personal responsibility and allowance of brutality showed itself clearly in the Ford Motor Company, where executives identifying with the first Henry Ford both submitted to and joined in with highly questionable behavior. Henry Ford had once been acclaimed not only as a mechanical genius, but also, after the announcement of the five-dollar day, as a philanthropist. Because of the darker sides of his actions, however, this image eventually changed. While the public merely ridiculed his endeavors in the social sphere, life inside the organization was not a laughing matter. The original champion of the working man became the tyrant of the Rouge plant, at that time the largest manufacturing facility in the world. Henry Ford's despotic one-man rule and continuous search for enemies increasingly had repercussions on every function of the company. Wall Street bankers, labor unions, and Jews turned into enemies, each group supposedly endangering his complete control over the company and obstructing him in his grandiose plans.

Under his chosen lieutenants-turned-henchmen— Liebold, Sorenson, and Bennett—blatant aggression became the norm and indiscriminate purges of employees for imagined offenses the order of the day. A system of intimidation aided by a large number of Detroit underworld characters, Bennett in particular, spread terror in the organization, a process originally instigated by Henry Ford himself. It was a period when organizational brutality reached an all-time high. In this case only new leadership, like the arrival of the grandson, Henry Ford II, was able to break the spell of the F-dimension.

In spite of our realization of the darker sides of leadership—its potential to induce regressive behavior leading to the abdication of personal responsibility—the desire for leadership seems here to stay. Freud was cognizant of humankind's need for leaders and noted, "We know that in the mass of mankind there is a powerful need for an authority who can be admired, before whom one bows down, by whom one is ruled and perhaps even ill-treated . . . that all the characteristics with which we equipped the great man are paternal characteristics. . . . The decisiveness of thought, the strength of will, the energy of action are part of the picture of a father . . . but above all the autonomy and independence of the great man, his divine unconcern which may grow into ruthlessness. One must admire him, one must trust him, but one cannot avoid being afraid of him too."

Freud compared the development of the bond between leader and followers to the act of falling in love. The followers somehow turn into sleepwalkers intoxicated by the leader. When these identification processes occur, followers indulge in an "orgy" of simple and strong emotions and may be swept along by the leader's appeal.

Although Freud did not mention it explicitly in the context of leadership, at the heart of this psychological process is a dynamic called transference, an exchange closely tied to projection that is really some kind of psychological confusion about the other person, a mysterious psychological mix-up in time and place. In interpersonal relationships, individuals repeat past patterns of interaction in the present, and in the process many regressive forces come into play. Leaders are ideal outlets for these transference reactions. However, not all leaders can handle such pressures and thus they are swept away by the F-dimension, as I will show in the next chapter.

3

The Mysterious Transformation: Leaders Who Can't Manage

*But his soul was mad. Being alone in
the wilderness, it had looked within itself,
and, by heavens! I tell you, it had gone
mad. I had—for my sins, I suppose—to
go through the ordeal of looking into it
myself. No eloquence could have been
so withering to one's belief in mankind
as his final burst of sincerity.*

Joseph Conrad, *Heart of Darkness*

L ooking back, many who had been acquainted with Robert Clark realized that discordant words had rarely been spoken about him—that is, before he assumed the presidency of the Solan Corporation, a company in the heavy equipment field. Robert had always been very well liked. His superiors had been impressed by his capacity for work, his dedication, and his imaginative way of tackling problems. And in spite of having the drive to get things done at work, he had seemed to be a genuinely nice person, always prepared to help and ready to spend time with those who asked.

From the moment Robert entered the company he had been recognized as someone destined to go far. And the soothsayers had not been off the mark. To the delight of many, he had crowned his seemingly brilliant career by being selected to succeed the old CEO. Excitement had filled the air in the period immediately after Robert took over, and he had received quite a few accolades for his role in taking a number of long overdue steps. He had approved a reorganization of the regional sales force and given the go-ahead for a new performance appraisal system. But, as many of his old colleagues later reflected, some time after he took charge, a transformation in his personality had seemed to take place. It was hard to describe in precise terms what had really happened. But whatever it was, most felt it was not a turn for the better.

The first sign that something was changing in Robert was his greater inaccessibility. Some wondered what had happened to his once widely acclaimed open-door policy and his statements about wanting to be a "hands-on" manager. But that was not all. What about his notions of participative management? They all seemed to have gone down the drain. Instead, he became increasingly authoritarian, impatient, and careless of the feelings of others.

Robert's aloof, authoritarian behavior spelled problems for the company. In their desire to please him, his key executives would jostle for his attention and spend time and energy on power games and intracompany squabbles rather than on strategic decisions. Outside market forces were neglected in favor of fulfilling political ambitions. Morale sank to an all-time low. And as could be expected, the financial results were dismal.

This scenario is not all that farfetched. An executive who to all appearances seems bright, likeable, and well adjusted reaches the top of an organization and increasingly resorts to strange behavior. Why he or she is suddenly behaving differently seems inexplicable to others in the company. It comes as a great surprise to all.

Of course, not all new leaders change when they reach the top; they don't have to behave according to Lord Acton's famous dictum, "Power corrupts and absolute power corrupts absolutely." On the contrary, many new leaders do very well. They manage to handle the pressures that leadership brings. Their way of steering the company may lead to revitalization and transformation. And the enthusiasm of a new CEO may be contagious, motivating subordinates to do things beyond normal expectations. Sometimes individuals who have been rather colorless before may even turn into great leaders when they attain a position of power.

Unfortunately, however, history has also provided us with examples of the opposite extreme: leaders whose behavior became pathological once they had attained power. We only have to think about political leaders such as the biblical King Saul, Rome's Caligula, King Ludwig of Bavaria, Hitler, Colonel Gadhafi, or business leaders such as the first Henry Ford or Howard Hughes. Of course, I am not suggesting that the average business leader will resort to pathological behavior upon reaching the top of his or her organization. However, to a greater or lesser extent, some leaders do seem to undergo a mysterious transformation on attaining power. Some leaders become the victim of the F-dimension. Before they take over, such leaders may come across as very likeable, well-adjusted persons, but they seem to undergo a sudden change when they rise to the top. To understand why this can happen we need to take a further look at the regressive forces that can affect leaders and followers. Some leaders are simply unable to cope with the pressures involved.

A FALSE CONNECTION

Leaders fulfill many functions, the most important one being to articulate to their followers a vision of the future of whatever task they try to accomplish and the means to get there. But apart from being catalysts to achieve the objectives of their organization through product market selection, resource procurement and allocation, competitive initiatives, administrative choices, and other forms of action, leaders take on additional functions, an important one being the symbolic role of "container." As I described in the last chapter, through projective processes—that is, the attribution to another of ideas that belong to oneself—leaders inadvertently become the recipients of their subordinates' ideals, wishes, feelings, and fantasies. And subordinates, by transforming subjective into objective reality, attribute to leaders mystical, charismatic powers. This may occur in spite of attempts on the leader's part to resist. What happens—and we have to remember that this is usually not a conscious process—is that some kind of false connection takes place in the minds of the subordinates. Followers may become confused when dealing with their leaders: they may perceive them and respond to them not according to the facts of the situation but as though the leader were a significant figure from their past such as a parent, other caretaker, or sibling. When this happens the boundaries between past and present disappear. It is easy to see that the attitudes, fantasies, and feelings that were appropriate in the conditions that prevailed in a person's early relationships can become inappropriate and anachronistic when they resurface in the context of the present.

To take an example: Howard Kent, president of Arctos Inc., a corporation in the snow removal equipment business, was surprised when inexplicably during a small advertising meeting one of his subordinates, Lise Clair, accused him of being prejudiced against women. He was rather dis-

34

turbed by this remark, particularly in light of the fact that he had gone out of his way to bring more women into executive positions. He let the comment be. Later in the day, however, he was visited by Lise, who apologized. She mentioned that she had given much thought to her outburst and was reminded of the fact that in her family her brother had always been favored. Although she had been a bright child, unlike her brother, she had never been encouraged to go on to a university. It had been an uphill struggle to get her parents to help her finance her college education. She wondered if the outburst at the meeting was related to the many fights she had had with her parents to get equal treatment.

As authority figures, leaders are prime outlets for these types of emotional reactions. As we saw, leaders easily revive in their followers previously unresolved conflicts with significant figures from the past. Such exchanges lead to regressive behavior. For example, followers may endow their leaders with the same magic powers and omniscience that in childhood they attributed to parents or other significant figures.

This tendency to modify and distort the whole context of relationships, or transference, is present in all meaningful interactions. Although it may be hard to accept this, all interpersonal exchanges seem to be a mixture of realistic *and* transference reactions. And leaders, in particular, are susceptible to this kind of confusion.

Transference reactions can be acted out in several ways and affect both leaders and followers. One common manifestation is for followers to *idealize* the leader in an attempt to recreate the sense of security and importance they felt in early childhood when being cared for by an apparently omnipotent and perfect parent. As an authority figure, a leader fits easily into the subconscious in a parent role. Subordinates therefore may be tempted to endow a leader in their minds with quite unrealistic powers and attributes; this in turn can inflate the leader's own self-esteem.

Particularly during periods of organizational upheaval —cutbacks or dramatic expansion—subordinates cling to their belief in a leader's powers as a way of maintaining their sense of security and identity. And in order to have a leader respond to their needs, subordinates often go out of their way to please or charm him or her, even giving in to extravagant whims or flights of fancy. In times of organizational crisis, a danger therefore exists that the leader may be surrounded by yes-men. This lack of critical review in decision making can obviously have dire consequences for the organization.

In the case of *mirror* transference, we are dealing with the other side of the coin. This involves humans' love of self-display, our desire to get attention from others. And although this inclination tends to be universal, leaders are more susceptible to it than most people. It is very hard to imagine, unless one has had the experience, what it means to be the target of excessive admiration by followers, even in those instances where some of it may be warranted. When this happens, the leader's display of narcissism reverberates in the followers. Followers recognize themselves in the leader. Some leaders, in being exposed to a great deal of attention, eventually find it hard to maintain a firm grasp on reality and thus distinguish fact from fancy. Too much admiration can have dire consequences for the leader's mind: he or she may eventually believe it all to be true— that he or she really is as perfect, as intelligent, or as powerful as others think is the case—and act accordingly. Moreover, the fact that leaders have something going for them that ordinary mortals don't have—the power to turn some of their fantasies into reality—may intensify this belief. If this happens, we may see the beginning of a self-propelled cycle of grandiosity. Eventually, such leaders end up living in a hall of mirrors.

Also bringing such wishes to the fore is the fact that at the base of the mirror transference is an archaic memory of grandiose omnipotence, a remembrance of a time when the individual as a child wanted to display his or her evolving capabilities and be admired for them. For the leader to experience this grandiose sense of self, he or she needs others to provide nourishment through confirming and admiring responses. Thus the idealizing and mirror transference reactions become complementary processes.

If leaders fall victim to these regressive forces and the F-dimension takes over, they may become overly preoccupied with fantasies of unlimited success and power. They will be constantly on the lookout for attention and may want to demonstrate their mastery and brilliance. Encouraged by their subordinates, they may take on overly ambitious projects and engage in unrealistic action. And because of their desire for grandiosity, they will tend to gravitate toward subordinates with high dependency needs, people in search of an all-knowledgeable, all-powerful, and care-giving leader. But the followers may be in for a shock. Preoccupied by grandiosity, and having become intolerant of criticism, such leaders can become very callous about the needs of their subordinates. They may exploit them and then drop them when they no longer serve their purposes.

Subordinates may legitimately react angrily to such behavior. However, another, less obvious, process may also be at work: subordinates may subconsciously blame their leader for failing to live up to their own exaggerated expectations. Angry about this, and perhaps aggravated by callous, exploitative behavior, they may quickly turn from admiration to hostility and rebellion. Like children, such people recognize no middle of the road, and tend to split all experiences, perceptions, and feelings into unambiguously "good" and "bad" categories. Of course, in doing so they ignore the complexity and ambiguity inherent in all human relationships; they refuse to accept that the same person can have both good and bad qualities. Thus, although a new leader may initially have been welcomed as a messiah, he or she may be surprised to find out how suddenly the followers' mood can shift. After one setback, followers may view their leader as responsible for all the company's problems, even if these long predate the leader's arrival.

Faced with a change from admiration to apparent rebellion and anger on the part of their followers, leaders may become irritated, having slight *persecutory* feelings. Of course, it is much easier to deal with admiration than to cope with being the target of aggressive feelings. But leaders have to realize that some of that is inevitable. This being the case, a certain amount of self-control is required. Some may be tempted, however, to retaliate; firing the critics is an obvious reaction. Some leaders tend to see their subordinates as belonging to one of two camps: those who are with them and those who are against them. The former can do no wrong and the latter no right, and an organizational culture of fear and suspicion is the likely outcome.

Subordinates who are with their leaders better have the same points of view and support them even if they engage in unrealistic, grandiose schemes or imagine the existence of malicious plots, sabotage, and enemies. It's no wonder that paranoia is considered to be one of the major diseases of leadership. Effective leaders, however, know how to contain their excessive emotional reactions and avoid being caught up, being less susceptible to the F-dimension.

To examine the effect of the F-dimension, let us consider the following incident. Due to the sudden unexpected death of his predecessor, Ted Howell was appointed as the new president of Larix Corporation, a company in the electronics equipment field. Ted had been recruited with the help of a headhunter who had highly recommended him. Previously, he had held a senior staff position in a company in the same line of business. A key factor in convincing the board to take him on had been Ted's knowledge of the industry.

When Ted assumed his responsibilities, many welcomed him as the long-awaited messiah, the charismatic hero who was expected to turn the tottering Larix Corporation around. Under the previous regime the company had been in the red for a number of years. Something had to be done now to reverse the situation.

Soon after his arrival, members of the board saw signs that Ted was having difficulty in dealing with the pressures of the job. A number of rash decisions made in his first week at the office were the first indications of trouble. But in spite of these mistakes, everything initially turned out better than expected. First, Ted had a lucky break in that one of the company's main competitors went out of business. This freed up an important segment of the market.

39

In addition, one of his subordinates came up with an excellent marketing idea, which he quickly adopted as his own and which proved to be very successful. True enough, some executives were bothered by the fact that their colleague never received credit for it. But whatever could be said about this, both factors helped to get Larix back into the black.

This success, unfortunately, seemed to go to Ted's head. He didn't recognize how lucky he had been. After the turnaround, he thought everything was possible. Somehow, he seemed to imagine he was like the mythical King Midas, turning everything into gold. Making a considerable show of it, Ted embarked on a dramatic expansion program, ignoring cautionary remarks made by subordinates, consultants, and bankers. And as if this was not enough, Ted took steps to move the company's headquarters to what he thought were more suitable surroundings, and to acquire an expensive company plane. Not surprisingly, these actions put a heavy strain on the company's finances. Those executives who disagreed or expressed their concern about these new moves found themselves fired. Consultants who suggested that Ted change course suffered the same fate. In the end, only those executives inclined toward sycophantic behavior, willing to share his grandiose ideas and satisfied by identifying with the aggressive side of him, accepting his hostile outbursts but also acting aggressively to others, remained. As expected, the unrealistic, overblown plans and the high expenditures put the company back into the red. Ted, however, was unwilling to admit his role in all this. When questioned at directors' meetings, he would become defensive and deny any responsibility for the losses. Instead, he would blame them on faulty moves made by his predecessor or on vindictive action by a number of executives who were "fortunately" no longer in his employ. He claimed that there were still some "rotten apples" in the company, but he would soon get rid of them. In his opinion, a turnaround was just around the corner. To an increasing number of members of the board, however, Ted's behavior was becoming unacceptable. Eventually, having become impatient with the continuing losses and Ted's imperious, paranoid behavior, they managed to remove him.

As in the case of Robert Clark, what we can see happening here is that an individual, apparently perfectly adjusted and capable in his previous job, is promoted, but when subjected to the various pressures of the new job as a leader, starts to behave irrationally and falls victim to the F-dimension. Why did Ted Howell behave like this?

One explanatory factor may have been the excessively high expectations placed upon Ted by his subordinates. Overwhelmed by all the attention he suddenly received, he may have allowed his sense of reality to become marred. And perhaps because of his inability to withstand these psychological pressures, he may have assumed that some of the qualities ascribed to him were true and behaved accordingly. Getting more applause turned into a major preoccupation for him. When, as expected, his grandiose actions backfired and he was unable to deliver, some of his subordinates reacted with anger. Ted retaliated, however, showing signs of paranoid behavior, and started to put blame on others. Only the ones who completely identified with him survived.

The distortive reaction patterns that I have described and that contribute to the strange, irrational behavior we sometimes find in leaders is what the F-dimension is all

41

about. These reaction patterns are semidormant tendencies with which we all have to deal. They revive easily in situations of leadership. And as I have indicated, some people find it very difficult to withstand their pressures, and eventually fall victim to the F-dimension.

This leads us to ask what other pressures leaders have to deal with. Do other elements contribute to the F-dimension?

ISOLATION FROM REALITY

On June 18, 1982, the body of Roberto Calvi, chairman of BANCO Ambrosiano, Italy's largest private bank, also called "the Bank of Priests" because of its close links with the Vatican, was found hanging under Blackfriars Bridge in London. Although the exact circumstances of his death will probably never be known, this was a very ignominious ending for one of Italy's most prominent bankers. It was also one of the saddest outcomes of Italy's biggest scandal, involving illegal bank transactions, a secret Masonic-style lodge named P2, the Mafia, and the Italian Secret Service. An investigation revealed that BANCO Ambrosiano was heavily in debt. Moreover, hundreds of millions of dollars were missing.

The extent of Calvi's involvement is not clear. He certainly carried a heavy responsibility in the matter. His secretive, control-oriented management style didn't help, and his remoteness was an added complication. When things came to a head, he must have been under tremendous strain. The Bank of Italy wanted an explanation for the extremely high exposure of loans. The stock exchange was pushing him to reveal the bank's major shareholders, a factor he was trying to conceal, having created ghost companies to acquire de facto control over the bank. Creditors were calling for money. Michele Sindona, a shady Sicilian financier who was later convicted of extortion, fraud, perjury, and misappropriation of funds both in Italy and the United States, was making threats. People once considered friends at the Vatican and in the Christian Democratic establishment were deserting him in droves or maneuvering to have him replaced. Then there was the blackmail by those providing him with "protection," his sentence for illegal capital exports, and various other judicial investigations that were snowballing.

From the newspaper accounts we get a picture of a man ill at ease at social events, not a person for small talk. Roberto Calvi was described as the most private of Catholic financiers, an individual who was very reserved and formal; communicating with him was a difficult task. From various descriptions, he seems to have been a person who would internalize his problems rather than confide in anyone.

Without question, the events that led up to the final denouement were dramatic, but even so, did it have to end the way it did? Didn't Calvi have another choice? Couldn't he have solved his problems in some other manner? Or was the whole affair even more serious—a case of foul play?

We cannot really give answers to these questions. We don't know Calvi's motives for acting the way he did. What we do know, however, is that in spite of a large number of executives reporting to him, he seemed to have ended up very much alone in dealing with his problems. The various reports indicate that he had no one to turn to, and this seems paradoxical in light of his contacts and his very active life. Unfortunately, this kind of isolation in a sea of people seems to be all too common among people at the top of organizations. And such isolation can affect their sense of reality and consequently lead to manifestation of the F-dimension.

The phrase "loneliness of command" has been used frequently in the context of leadership. But is this a realistic concept? Is it an illusion created by leaders when, in fact, they may need no one? Is it a platitude, or is there something very real about it? Actually, it may be better to speak of the loneliness of command in the context of isolation from reality. The inability to test our perceptions, the tendency to lose touch with reality, is a danger anyone can fall victim to when in a position of leadership.

For example, when Peter Harris took up the position of president of the Noro Corporation he expected business to go on as usual. He imagined that not much would change in his lifestyle, that he would continue working much as he had before. The appointment had been very much a routine one. As one of the senior vice-presidents of his company he had been the logical choice for the job.

Events, however, turned out to be quite different. Peter had to deal with more changes in his lifestyle than he had expected. Soon after he assumed the presidency he realized that in spite of his efforts to maintain the same amicable operating mode, he was creating distance between himself and his subordinates. Although he tried for a while to be one of the boys, he discovered that this was no longer possible. Things had changed.

For example, there were his activities after work. He remembered how much he used to enjoy having a drink with his colleagues. He had always seen it as an ideal opportunity to let off steam. And it had other advantages. Many times, a quiet chat over a drink had helped him solve a knotty problem. But now, somehow, it had become harder to do. He had even dropped his weekly tennis game with an old-time colleague. As an explanation he had used the worn-out pretext of having too much work. The unstated but real reason was that both had felt increasingly uncomfortable in continuing their old relationship. At the heart of the matter was Peter's difficulty in socializing with and having to make tough career decisions about the same person. Life seemed much simpler if he retained some distance. And adding to his change in attitude was the discovery that friendliness to a subordinate was quickly interpreted by others as favoritism; attempts at closeness by a subordinate were similarly seen as a lobbying effort.

Although by keeping his distance he simplified matters, it didn't come without a price. He found his new way of behaving very frustrating. He increasingly felt a sense of isolation, a loss of intimacy. Somehow, he felt left out, cut off. Of course, he had his wife to talk to. But that didn't seem to be enough. She was busy with her own work, and she had her own things to worry about. He would have liked to confide in someone more familiar with what happened in the business, someone on whom he could test his ideas.

Sometimes, nostalgically, he would think of old times, the period before he became president. Everything had seemed to be so much simpler and easier. He remembered the fun he had had exchanging thoughts and ideas with his colleagues. And he recalled how he could always go to his president for help. But when he had become president himself his whole fabric of social interaction had been disturbed. Occasionally, he found himself longing for a way to resurrect the broken network of relationships, searching for a way of sharing. But it was just impossible. A side effect of it all was that he found himself becoming increasingly irritated about having gotten himself into this position. It was not what he had expected. It made him wonder to what extent his increasing aloofness was affecting his ability to make sensible decisions.

What can we learn from this example and that of Roberto Calvi? How does the F-dimension get into the picture again?

As I have indicated before, in organizations a major leadership task is to take care of the existing strategic and structural needs. Leaders are supposed to articulate a vision of the future and show how to get there. But as we have seen, leadership has a number of other aspects. One of these is to take care of the dependency needs of subordinates. But given the universal nature of these needs, the question then becomes: Who takes care of the dependency needs of the leaders themselves? Attachment needs also apply to them. When, as often happens, there is nobody to take care of these needs, anxiety associated with loneliness may come to the fore. Accompanying feelings are those of longing and disconnectedness. Basic separation anxiety—the awareness of abandonment—may be reactivated.

Some leaders, when they reach the top, discover to their great dismay that their network of complex mutual dependencies has been disturbed. Many leaders are able to overcome this and find other forms of gratification. Some may even have a mind-set that is counterdependent, actually favoring detached behavior. This kind of compatibility between personal makeup and position is not, however, the rule. Instead, some leaders become upset at finding themselves in this situation, and react accordingly. A very common response is one of anger, a desire for revenge for feeling left out. This is based on a seemingly irrational desire to blame others for not gratifying one's dependency needs. This isolation from reality and scapegoating behavior may contribute to a very politicized organizational culture, creating problems of coordination because of interdepartmental rivalry.

Aggression, however, can also be turned inward, leading to the kind of extreme depressive reactions we saw in the case of Roberto Calvi. Substance abuse such as alcoholism or drug taking may accompany such reactions. Again, we see the emergence of the F-dimension. Predictably, if such extreme responses to frustration of dependency needs continue, they can have dire consequences for the organization.

THE FEAR OF SUCCESS

In a society oriented toward success, failure is looked on as a catastrophe, and to some extent we all fear it. But while the fear of failure as a reactivating mechanism for feelings of insufficiency and incompetence is much more understandable, the phenomenon known as the fear of success is more of a mystery. In fact, many years ago, Freud tried to demystify some of the dynamics behind this fear in an article called "Those Wrecked by Success." He noted that some people become sick when a deeply rooted and long-cherished desire comes to fulfillment. He gave as example a professor who cherished a wish to succeed his teacher. When eventually this wish came true and the individual succeeded his mentor, depression, feelings of self-depreciation, and work inhibition set in.

The explanation of this phenomenon seems to be that to some people success becomes symbolically equated with an "Oedipal triumph," a victory in doing better than the parents of childhood. This is particularly true for those individuals who have never satisfactorily resolved rivalrous feelings toward parents and siblings. If this is the case, to be successful (measured in many different ways such as power, love, and money) and to have tangible accomplishments can turn into a pyrrhic victory. It is both wanted and feared.

At the heart of the problem is the fact that success makes people stand out and be noticed. Being in such a position may arouse the envy and resentment of others. Thus, retaliation will be feared from the person with whom one is competing. Hence—and we have to remember this is usually an unconscious, symbolic process—success may be transformed into some kind of hostile act against shadows from the past. Guilt and retribution are to be expected.

Thus, we can observe how in certain instances leaders who suffer from the fear of success may do very well until they reach a top position. Then, suddenly, having been finally successful in their aggressive strivings, they may become anxious, deprecate their achievements, and even engage in self-defeating behavior.

Ex-President Nixon seems to be a good case in point here: a political leader who, it seemed, unconsciously needed to fail in order to appease his guilt. Much has already been made of how his family, composed of a myth-making mother who would create a reality suited to her needs, and a rather brutal father who would use physical means to obtain obedience, affected his particular way of acting. Of course, with the advantage of knowing his background, we find some of Nixon's actions less remarkable. Here was a leader who demonstrated great political acumen, and who also possessed a remarkable ability to exploit the baser needs of the American public. His vicious anti-Communist campaigns and his investigation of the Alger Hiss affair are examples of these abilities. He was also a leader who had the strength and ability to turn major defeats into mere setbacks. His personal background seems to have made him very skilled at withstanding the rough-and-tumble of the political arena. But in spite of all his talents and his eventual achievements, Nixon repeatedly managed "to snatch defeat out of the jaws of victory." We can see this in the way he resorted to easily discovered small lies when talking to the press, in his secret slush fund in the 1952 presidential campaign, and finally, of course, in the Watergate cover-up.

Sometimes we can see how top executives fall victim to this form of anxiety. To take an example: Reflecting on his career, Ted Nolan recalled that it had come as quite a surprise to him when he was asked to succeed Larry Fulton as president of the Dalton Corporation. Like many of his colleagues, he had thought that the VP of marketing was the person most likely to be selected by the board. But, to use his own words, he certainly didn't protest when asked, and felt excitement at having the opportunity to crown his career at Dalton in the top job. When his appointment came through he was slightly ill at ease, however—a feeling that didn't go away when he took over the reins. He became increasingly preoccupied with the question of whether he could hack it. Would he be able to execute his responsibilities? Would he sound believable to his subordinates? He began to have difficulty sleeping at night, tormenting himself over whether his decisions of the previous day had been correct. Even worse, he had nightmares, dreaming about such crazy things as lions running after him or his being forced to enter lions' dens. Often he also felt like an impostor who was lucky to get the job. He also, he was later able to admit, developed a full-fledged drinking problem. He found it increasingly difficult to concentrate and make decisions at work. And he wondered how many of his problems in handling the CEO job were noticed by his board members. When were they going to realize that they had made a mistake and that he was really incapable and a fake?

However, he was fortunate. His wife was a great support to him. Because of the changes in his behavior, she became concerned and encouraged him to see a psychotherapist, something he would never have done on his own. His visits to the psychotherapist were very fruitful. Together, they began to explore the underlying causes of his anxiety. The therapist made him realize that all his life he had been quite anxious every time he was put in a position of responsibility. Previously, however, he had been able to handle it better, since there had always been others in a similar situation with whom he could talk. But this time, he was really on his own and, as he said, the buck stops here. There was nowhere to hide!

With the help of the psychotherapist, he discovered the relationship between where he came from and his present feelings. In reviewing his life, he realized how successful he had been, having overcome tremendous handicaps to work himself up to a position far above his parents and siblings. But he also recognized that with this success had come feelings of betrayal of his origins and a deep sense of guilt. Having risen so far above his roots seemed to have contributed to his present state of anxiety. He explored these feelings with his psychotherapist and succeeded in bringing greater reality to the situation by integrating the feelings with his present life situation. Being able to see those connections, going through the repetitive process of working through those insights, brought him a greater peace of mind. In ending his reflections, Ted felt he was now doing a pretty good job at the office. He certainly had no problem making decisions any longer.

Nixon and Nolan are examples of persons whose dangerous inner images made the F-dimension operative. Other psychological scenarios can be found, although the final outcome is usually the same. For instance, there is the individual who unconsciously equates success (in whatever form) with giving in to others, usually to parents. The parents may have wanted to gratify their own narcissistic needs vicariously through the accomplishments of their children. Parents who do this put formidable pressure on the child to succeed. Some children, however, may rebel against being made into a proxy, against having to participate in "mission impossible." In an otherwise inexplicable way they fall back on self-defeating behavior and self-sabotage the moment they become successful.

Some leaders may undo their success for the simple reason that their own dependency needs have become too pressing. Again, this is usually not a conscious act; the stress of being in a position of power may be too overwhelming. Success brings greater responsibilities and a change in comfortable routines. Also, symbolically, success

51

may mean the annihilation of one's old identity. Some leaders find it very hard to handle these changes. Thus, the deliberate attempt to fail is actually a cry for help.

THE QUESTION OF SUSCEPTIBILITY

We have seen how transference reactions, the loneliness of command, and the fear of success are all different aspects of the F-dimension. An obvious question follows: Are certain types of leaders more susceptible to the F-dimension than others? This in turn brings up questions of how to distinguish different leadership styles. What are the differentiating features? Are certain leadership styles more common in contemporary society than others? What are the danger signs among the different types?

4

The Spectrum of Personalities: Leaders and Followers

The capacity to be ruthless, driving and immoral, if also combined with intelligence and imagination can be a winning combination in politics as well as commerce. . . . Sociopathic and paranoid personality traits that are most dangerous in people in power are precisely those characteristics most suitable for the attainment of power in a competitive culture such as ours.

Willard Gaylin, *New York Times Magazine*

As Willard Gaylin points up, finding a yardstick to judge the personality styles of leaders is not easy. Traits of character that would be considered aberrant in ordinary circumstances may provide the ingredients of success for someone in a leadership position. Nevertheless, individuals showing such traits are always in greater danger of succumbing to the regressive pressures described in the last chapter, and hence to dysfunctional leadership styles. Meanwhile, certain specific characteristics make an individual less likely to be a leader at all, and may instead condition him or her to be a follower.

Which, then, are the personality characteristics likely to typify successful leaders? What are the characteristics that contribute to the F-dimension? Finally, what are the characteristics that make people more suitable to be followers?

In understanding behavior we should realize that both leaders and followers are engaged in a metaphorical way in some form of theater. This theater contains specific scenarios, the bases of which are imagined, desired, and feared relationships between the individual and significant others. These core conflictual relationship themes profoundly influence our affective and cognitive states and our behavior, and lead us to gravitate toward certain personality constellations. In these "stage activities," patterns of the past seem to be reenacted in the present. To use the words of Joyce McDougall, "Each secret-theatre self is . . . engaged in repeatedly playing roles from the past, using techniques discovered in childhood and reproducing, with uncanny precision, the same tragedies and comedies, with the same outcomes and an identical quota of pain and pleasure. What were once attempts at self-cure in the face of mental pain and conflict are now symptoms that the adult I produces, following forgotten childhood solutions."

The Diagnostic and Statistical Manual of Mental Disorders (DSM III-R) published by the American Psychiatric Association makes these stage activities more specific and classifies different personality syndromes into a number of types according to their various distinguishing characteristics. What follows is a brief look at some of these types, largely based on DSM III-R, and at the sort of leaders they produce. One of them, the narcissistic type, is so important in the study of leadership that I have devoted a whole chapter (Chapter 5) to it. For purposes of clarity, I describe a fairly extreme version of the different types. It should be realized, however, that the types are not simply types of mental disorders; each type includes the entire range of behavior from normal to dysfunctional, normality and pathology being relative concepts. Also, it should be recognized that in reality, most people are hybrids, showing a mixture of the various styles, with no single style being exaggerated to any significant extent. These styles, then, should be seen as worthwhile forms of shorthand in that they may help the observer to see certain elements of personality that are often not immediately noticed. In describing these personality dispositions, I expand the descriptions given in DSM III-R and refer to such elements as behavior, emotion, defensive structure, intrapsychic organization, and development.

THE AGGRESSIVE DISPOSITION

In the business world many examples can be found of individuals who show aspects of this style. *Fortune*'s annual list of the ten toughest bosses is a good illustration of an attempt to grapple with this dimension of leadership. The abrasive character of some CEOs has been legendary. Some particularly well known for their abrasiveness, their ruthlessness in dealing with their people as shown in their purges of their organizations, have been given nicknames like "Idi" or "neutron," reminders of the Ugandan tyrant or the neutron bomb, the latter as we know leaving in its wake only buildings, not people.

To take an example, Norman Lowell, the new CEO of the Baedeker Corporation, made things quite clear on his first day at work when he addressed his executive group. He outlined his program for change and told the assembled employees that if they disagreed with him they might as well pick up their paycheck right now and leave. With hindsight, many wished that they had listened and taken him up on it. It would have saved them much agony later on.

It didn't take long for the executive group to realize that Lowell meant business. One senior executive who questioned the wisdom of one of his orders got a dressing down he had not had since he was in boot camp, and found himself fired. Others were soon to follow. Lowell's abrasiveness and temper was very hard to take. His tongue lashings made most executives tremble and what was worse was that he seemed to get pleasure out of these scenes. For many executives the strain was much too much and they decided to leave of their own volition, so that they would, as they put it, "no longer have to face that SOB" and could "get on with living." But whatever could be said about Lowell's particular way of acting, the short-term results for the company didn't look all that bad. However, given the loss of so many good people, some wondered if these good results could continue.

People like Lowell come across as socially forceful and intimidating. They pride themselves on their self-reliance, fearlessness, unsentimentality, and hard-boiled competitive values; tradition, humanistic concerns, and social compassion are not important to them. They like to portray themselves as tough-minded, not in need of anyone.

Such individuals are very energetic, competitive, and power-oriented, not concerned about threats or punitive action. Their behavior probably contains a counterphobic element—that is, it is a way of mastering their fears. Thus, such people sincerely believe that the world is a jungle; one has to be the aggressor to keep the upper hand.

The central theme characterizing all aggressive behavior is the expectation that others will be hostile, thus justifying the aggressor's mistrustful and aggressive attitudes. Aggressive individuals believe in protective reaction; misguided self-protection encourages them to strike first. They see most others as devious, controlling, and punitive. The advantage of viewing the world in this way is that it helps absolve them of feelings of shame and guilt about their own often irresponsible actions. Having diverted these feelings, they act recklessly and impulsively. They justify anger and vengeful behavior as a preemptive counterattack.

The extent to which aggressive people dominate others and seem to obtain satisfaction in doing so is striking. Others are regarded as means to an end, to be used and frightened into submission, and because of this, aggressors feel that everything is permitted; this gives their behavior a very unpleasant quality. They tend to possess a temper that flares quickly into argument and counterattack; moreover, they often stand out because of their antisocial behavior. No wonder that these people are usually unable to sustain lasting, close relationships with others.

At work, aggressive types can be impulsive, very unpredictable, and even self-destructive. A planning mode is not for them. In light of their aggressive ways of dealing with others, job changes are quite common; they are also the type of person who will impulsively walk out of a job without having made provisions for another. Extreme cases will even refuse to accept social norms with respect to lawful behavior or fail to honor financial or other obligations.

Their rebelliousness and resistance to authority often make people of aggressive disposition very problematic followers. Given their desire for power and dominance, it is not surprising that this personality type is more commonly found in positions of leadership rather than followership. They pride themselves on being oriented toward the "bottom line." This orientation seems to warrant any form of action. And although they may have certain competencies, they lack one important quality necessary for effective leadership: the ability to create networks, to build alliances with others. People of this type who attain a leadership position may have suppressed or temporarily suspended aspects of their more abrasive side to enable their rise to the top. Once they reach a position of power, however, their abrasiveness may resurface.

At the origin of this kind of behavior we can usually find a history of parental rejection or hostility. For various reasons the child may have become a recipient of the displaced anger of the parents. As the most vulnerable within the family structure, the child becomes the easiest outlet for aggression. Hostility leads to more hostility and becomes the model for similar behavior later in life. With such a background, authority figures are not looked at as positive and benevolent but as tough, dangerous, and abusive. Such children as adults will have internalized this parental model of hostile interaction. Thus, they reject authority, but, paradoxically, are willing to take on positions of leadership and then abuse others.

THE PARANOID DISPOSITION

In March 1966, Captain Marcus Aurelius Arnheiter was relieved of command of the destroyer escort radar ship *USS Vance*, which was assigned to patrol the South Vietnamese coast in order to intercept infiltrators and smugglers of arms and ammunition. During his ninety-nine days of command the resemblance between his behavior and that of the fictional Queeg's command of the *Caine* had become uncanny. Propelled by a desire for fame that had been kindled by avid reading of C. S. Forester's Captain Horatio Hornblower novels in his youth combined with an admiration for Lord Nelson, the famous admiral of the Napoleonic wars, Arnheiter engaged in increasingly bizarre behavior. Gradually, paranoid reactions would seep through. He would violate regulations to get into the fire zone and send back false position reports. He would then shoot at sand dunes, chickens, sharks, and sea snakes, and give later embellished accounts of these activities, believing himself to have been persecuted by the enemy. Once he was so enthralled with the fighting action that he endangered the lives of his crew by forgetting that he had command of the bridge and was on a collision course with the rocks of a peninsula. He also hatched a mad plot to sink a Chinese submarine, an illegal act of war had he succeeded. His early morning spiritual harangues over the loudspeaker system, the enforcement of unrealistic dress codes, and the acquisition of a speedboat from the crew's recreation money to use in pursuit of the enemy were, not surprisingly, highly unpopular with his men. This behavior, coupled with his sending letters to the sailors' wives or parents warning them that he would court-martial their husbands or sons if they were caught again with a venereal disease, and the way in which he forced his officers to recommend him for a Silver Star, created an extremely mutinous atmosphere on his ship that finally came to the attention of higher command.

If one feature stands out in the behavior of people such as Arnheiter, it is their pervasive and unwarranted suspicion of other people. These people tend to misread the action of others, questioning their loyalty; they expect

61

trickery and deception everywhere. Their lack of trust is symptomized in an overconcern with hidden motives and special meanings, leading to a distortion in perceptions, thoughts, and memories. Even if no confirmation of their suspicions is found, they build them up into an intricate web indicating the deviousness of "the others."

Such individuals inflate themselves through the creation of grandiose and persecutory fantasies. They are hypervigilant, constantly scanning the environment for signs of threat, taking unnecessary precautions. Others perceive them as guarded and secretive. They tend to avoid accepting blame even where it is warranted. Such people deny personal weakness or responsibility. They are blind to their own faults and instead blame others. Splitting, the tendency to divide the world into two camps, and projection, blaming others for what originates within themselves, become their favorite defense mechanisms. With their intense, narrowly focused attention span and their hypervigilance, they search for confirmation of their biases, and as a consequence, are unable to take a dispassionate view of things. In their preoccupation with details they pay insufficient attention to the bigger picture.

Their hypersensitivity and hypervigilance make them difficult people to live with. They are quarrelsome and quick to take offense; they possess an abrasive irritability. Difficulties are easily exaggerated. They magnify and distort problems, making mountains out of molehills. Their hypersensitivity also leads to a readiness to counterattack, even when the threat is minimal. Being constantly on guard, they are continually tense, unable to relax.

In their emotional life these people appear restricted and cold. They falsely pride themselves on being objective, rational, and unemotional. A sense of humor is often lacking, as are passive, soft, tender, and sentimental feelings.

These people are often interested in mechanical devices, electronics, and automation. The reason for this fascination is that these devices may help them in monitoring their environment, warning them of any sign of threat. Needless to say, such alertness may be of benefit to an organization, but unfortunately these people find it hard to differentiate between a real and critical threat and an unimportant situation or event.

At the heart of this particular way of functioning usually lies an upbringing by extremely intruding parents. The developing child seems to be caught in a web of projections and attributions of others, making it very difficult to create his or her own psychic space. A great state of uncertainty about self and self in relation to others exists, and the child becomes confused about where his or her self ends and the other self begins. To arrive at some level of autonomy or individuation turns into an enormous struggle and often is looked at as an attack by the rest of the family. Thus persecutory feelings are very much a psychic reality. The earlier-mentioned interest in mechanical devices may actually symbolize a reaction against feelings of being controlled by uncontrollable forces. Thoughts of omnipotence and defensive, highly rigid ideas of self-importance become a way of fighting feelings of helplessness. And when under too much stress, this inflated bubble of self-importance can easily burst, leading to highly explosive reactions. Given the effects of all these forces, reality testing can be seriously impaired.

Individuals with this particular disposition are very cognizant of the dynamics of power. They carefully assess status and position and are envious and jealous of those at higher levels. Being in a leadership position seems to accentuate these characteristics. Naturally, the higher one goes, the more envy comes to the fore and the more vulnerable and sensitive one feels to attacks by others. It is no wonder that these tendencies become magnified when a paranoid individual gains power. Paranoia and leadership seem to be closely linked. Of course, when we see such behavior some predispositions must have already been there; in fact, the analytical focus of these people may actually have been congenial to their rise to the top. But with a position of leadership comes visibility, envy, and criticism, serving to accentuate dormant psychopathological tendencies. Inability to contain paranoid inclinations when in a leadership position is a very common cause of leadership failure.

And as we could see, Captain Arnheiter showed many characteristics of this style, seeing enemies everywhere. In this case, however, one factor made it harder to recognize his mad behavior—the fact that an element of reality existed: a war was going on. So we can see how in certain situations behavior that would otherwise be considered mad may become the norm.

THE HISTRIONIC DISPOSITION

Many of the colleagues of Anne Murphy, an account executive with a prominent advertising firm, felt that she had reached as responsible a position as she would ever get to in the company. According to them, a number of recent assignments of large accounts had been the giveaway. The general feeling was that her way of dealing with these more complex tasks had been unsatisfactory. All in all, her management of these situations had been too global, vague, and/or superficial, and sometimes even disjointed and illogical. For example, her summaries of important discussions were often highly indefinite, making it difficult to arrive at specific decisions. Moreover, she had a tendency to overreact to things. Frequently, she would give only glancing attention to details. Sometimes it would even be worse: she would completely forget important factors. Some of her colleagues had even concluded that Anne Murphy at times suspended clear, logical thinking and did not properly assess the complexity of the situation. Also bothersome was the fact that she tended to be too quick to lean on others and turn over responsibilities that were really hers. Furthermore, all too often, things seemed to just happen to her, without her appearing to have control over the situation.

But in spite of these negatives, most people did appreciate her. She certainly seemed to thrive in the environment of excitement and glamour that advertising tended to offer. She was always very sociable and seemed to make friends easily. As far as the latter were concerned it was perhaps better to talk of acquaintances, however, since most of these friendships appeared superficial. On the negative side, some male executives had been bothered by her tendency to behave seductively at times. She certainly managed to draw the attention of men without really understanding how or what she was doing. But if a reaction was forthcoming she was very quick to cut short any advances to her flirtations. She could be very flighty. All these characteristics made her a very likeable person, but not exactly material for future promotion.

People like Anne Murphy are propelled by a desperate need to attract attention at all costs. Their behavior thus becomes overdramatic and overemotional. Individuals who possess this particular style tend to be very reactive to external stimuli, ever alert to the desires and moods of others. Frequently, this makes for an incapacity to concentrate and an inability to focus attention sharply. Thus, such people's judgment is impressionistic and fleeting, not really based on the facts of the situation. This tendency to rely on what others think or feel, this wish to please and ingratiate, is symptomatic of the central theme that frames their inner theater: dependency and helplessness. Such people tend to be sociable, constantly looking for nurturance, reassurance, and protection. Their sense of self-worth seems to depend very much on the opinions of others. This wish for dependent relationships makes them very impressionable and easily influenced. They often use seduction, in any form, as a way of creating this type of relationship. At the same time, given their neediness, they can be very egocentric and self-indulgent, inconsiderate of the needs of others.

A number of other characteristics should also be mentioned. These people crave activity and excitement and consequently have a very low tolerance for delay, frustration, and disappointment. This can be a positive characteristic, as it makes for a proactive mode and helps to get things done. The negative side is that these people may overreact to minor events, acting on hunches and impressions. This emotional excitability can lead to irrational behavior, angry outbursts, or tantrums, and also to capricious action.

Moreover, often these people come across as shallow, lacking in genuineness, even if superficially they may appear warm and charming. To many it looks as if they are playing a part, not really dealing with substantive issues. Self-insight seems to be lacking. Somehow their emotions and cognitions are disconnected from consciousness, making for a quality of dissociation.

Naturally, individuals who act in this way respond very positively to anyone with strong authority whom they expect to offer magical solutions to their problems. This, combined with their incapacity for sustained concentration, their distractibility or impressionability, makes followership more common than leadership for this type. They don't usually have what it takes to assume a position of leadership. Still, some elements of this style, and here I am particularly thinking about the energy level that comes with it, mixed with another style like narcissism, can make for quite effective leadership.

The origin of this behavior seems to be difficulty as a growing child in capturing the attention and affection of the parents. Parents may give very little attention to their children's needs or deal with them merely as extensions of themselves. When that is the case, children discover quickly that only selected types of behavior will meet with parental approval. This irregular bestowal of attention can make for a lifelong search to elicit these rewards. To get attention, exaggeration of needs becomes imperative. The main objective becomes to get *any* reaction from the other, a behavior pattern not based on firmly entrenched values and beliefs.

THE DETACHED DISPOSITION

On February 3, 1975, Eli Black, rabbi by training and businessman by inclination, chairman, president, and CEO of United Brands, a two-billion-dollar multinational food company, smashed his attaché case through his office window on the forty-fourth floor of mid-Manhattan's Pan Am Building and leaped to his death. United Brands issued a statement saying that Mr. Black had been under "great strain during the past several weeks because of business pressures. He had been working 16–18 hours a day and had become severely depressed because of the tension."

The year 1974 had been a difficult one for the diversified banana and meat company. Hurricane damage, high cattle-feed costs, and increased banana export taxes had resulted in serious losses for the year, but the worst seemed to be over, according to many United Brands executives. Eli Black had negotiated his company through a tight financial squeeze and managed to overcome the various disasters that had occurred during the year. Some people who knew him suggested, however, that he may have been troubled by extortion demands and payment of a $1,250,000 bribe to a high Honduran official to have the banana tax lowered.

A descendant of ten generations of rabbis and scholars, Black had been ordained a rabbi himself and for four years had served a congregation on Long Island. But according to friends, he had felt his life as a rabbi to be unfulfilling. He had decided to leave and had joined Lehman Brothers, the investment house, going on to become chairman and CEO of the American Seal-Kap Corporation in 1954. He had succeeded in developing the tiny company through a series of acquisitions, eventually merging with United Fruits

68

Company in 1970. The giant company he had created was renamed United Brands.

According to some sources, Black ran his company in an erratic way. At some times he would rule with an iron hand, while at other times he would permit United Brands' different fiefdoms to operate seemingly autonomously. He would place a premium on his executives' loyalty, but would overrule them and play them off against each other, not permitting anyone to disagree with him.

Both business associates and friends described Mr. Black as a very reserved, formal man who "frequently smiled but rarely laughed," a person who never "broke his calm, controlled bearing enough to shout out in anger." Black does not seem to have been a person for small talk; indeed, he was known to be very difficult to communicate with. He was also someone who shunned the limelight. Only in 1973, after repeated badgering by his senior executives, did he finally permit a picture of himself to be shown in the annual report.

According to some of his senior executives at his Boston office, he had become increasingly "disoriented" over the past year. Power plays had been rampant in United Brands, with the Boston office as the center of a revolt that had been building up to open warfare. Some sources even mentioned that intense feuding at board meetings had given Black the feeling that he was going to be ousted.

We will never know the reason for Black's unfortunate act, but from his behavior and the descriptions of others we recognize elements of the detached style, and we can see how this style affected his entire organization.

Individuals more extreme than Black who possess the pure version of the detached personality style form another category described by DSM III-R. Such people may be subdivided into two separate groups: schizoid and avoidant. Schizoid individuals, the more severely dysfunctional of these two types, may have emotional or cognitive deficits that make them incapable of establishing close relationships; these people seem to be genuinely indifferent to others. In contrast, avoidant personalities are actively detached—that is, their detachment is of a more self-protective nature. Because of fears of interpersonal rejection or depreciation, they prefer to stay distant. The basis of this restraint is probably early childhood experiences of parental devaluation, rejection, and loss, of having the feeling that one is not wanted, or does not give pleasure to anyone, or may hurt the person to whom one feels attached. Another basis may be the fear of losing one's identity as a separate individual because of domination by another person. The surface behavior, however, is very much the same for the two groups. Both groups tend to be socially unresponsive. They tend to be very guarded, and are frightened of intimacy. Demonstrative feelings are absent.

Both types exhibit emotional coldness and aloofness, an absence of apparent warm, tender feelings for others. Although they may seem well adapted to organizational life, such individuals may also give the impression of not being involved. They seem to be unable to engage in the give and take of reciprocal relationships. They emanate an air of wanting privacy.

A bland exterior and the tendency to flatten emotional events are other characteristics. Avoidance and repression of feelings are accompanying patterns, as is indifference to praise or criticism or to the feelings of others.

Usually, it is difficult for this type of person to establish close relationships. They evince little apparent desire for social involvement, and restrict social relationships due to the fear that contacts may become disruptive and painful. They are loners, only willing to enter into relationships if given unusually strong assurances of uncritical acceptance.

The avoidant subgroup is hypersensitive to potential rejection, humiliation, and shame. Given their low self-esteem, they quickly interpret innocuous events as ridicule. But at the same time, given their deep-seated desire for affection and acceptance, they are distressed by their inability to relate comfortably to others. They are far too afraid, however, to become strongly attached and dependent. To do so would make rejection even more devastating.

Finally, these people feel alienated from themselves and others. They may resort to fantasy as a flight from painful reality. They may even feel that their behavior has a mechanical quality; that they are just going through the motions, not really feeling alive. To the outside world they present a mask or a "false self." In interpersonal encounters they sometimes act as if they are not there. They often have an air of vagueness about them, a behavior pattern accentuated by defective, fearful, perceptual scanning.

It is predictable that people possessing these qualities may experience serious difficulties both in the role of leader and follower. To work for a leader with these characteristics is not easy. The relationship of Howard Hughes to the Hughes empire is probably an extreme example of such an interface, apart from the paranoid aspects that also characterized his style. While Eli Black could probably to some extent take on the "container" role, people such as Howard Hughes are unable to do so. They don't have the

71

capacity to take care of the emotional needs of others, which is one of the qualities that characterizes effective leaders. Followers find it highly frustrating not to know what is expected of them and not to receive any feedback about accomplishments. The detached individual's lack of social warmth and genuine involvement usually limits his or her chances of attaining leadership. Only occasionally, when another executive is present who is willing to take care of the emotional needs of subordinates, can such a leadership style succeed. Otherwise, only a mixture of this style with another one can make for some success in leadership. As a rule, these people find it easier to occupy a more subordinate position in an organization, and even then, their social detachment often makes them useful only for specific functions.

THE CONTROLLING DISPOSITION

Gustav Krupp von Bohlen und Halbach, the consort of Bertha, nicknamed the "Cannon Queen," certainly stood out because of his highly unusual behavior. In running the giant German armaments company, his management style could best be compared to that of a machine. He behaved like the ultimate martinet. After his marriage to Bertha Krupp, the sole heiress of the Krupp concern, having now become responsible for the management of the firm, he embraced as a long-lost friend the *Generalregulativ* (the general regulation) written and introduced by his forceful predecessor, Alfred. What Gustav lacked in imagination and foresight he found in this constitution, which described in unusual detail the rights and responsibilities of all his workers, the "Kruppianer." For a man whose vacation pastime was reading railroad timetables, this passion to make the *Generalregulativ* his bible was not surprising. His love for record keeping seems to have been unsurpassed, as was his fascination with the stopwatch. In all of his actions, an expectation of obedience stood central: not only obedience of his Kruppianer to the letter of the *Generalregulativ* but also his own blind obedience to the idea of what the House of Krupp stood for. This continued in his later misguided obedience to the leader of the Third Reich. His unquestioning attitude made the company infamous for its use of slave labor during World War II. For Gustav, trivia replaced substance; ritual took over from content.

A good illustration of his preoccupations is given by William Manchester in *The Arms of Krupp*: "Visitors weren't allowed to come in their own cars; their chauffeurs might be lax. Under the regulation drill, Krupp drivers dropped them off at the main entrance at 1:29 p.m. At 1:30 they entered the reception room to chat with Gustav and Bertha until 1:40, when they were led into the dining room. The moment Krupp finished a course, servants removed all plates from the table; poky or garrulous eaters were left hungry. The meal ended at 2:15, coffee at 2:29. At 2:30 on the dot the guests stepped into the waiting limousines and were driven away. Nothing was left to chance, including the temperature of the coffee, which might have thrown everything out of whack and which, therefore, was never too hot."

Obviously, the central theme in the life of people like Gustav Krupp von Bohlen und Halbach is control. More than anything else, these people want to control all the things that affect their lives. They want the world to be an ordered, disciplined place where everything is predictable. Their preoccupation with control can be seen as their way of managing their hostile feelings toward the ones who have been controlling them. Reaction formation, isolation of feelings, repetitive behavior, undoing, and intellectualization become defensive mechanisms to keep their hostile impulses and contrary inclinations in check. And their hostility can go two ways: it can take the route of submission or tyranny. Parental overcontrol is usually to blame for such behavior. The growing child learns to operate within the approved boundaries set by the parents, fearful to deviate or take initiative, given the dreaded sanctions against acting out of line. But such an upbringing leaves a legacy of irritation and resentment.

Excessive emotional control and a restricted ability to express warm and tender feelings are what differentiates these individuals from others. Spontaneous emotional responsiveness is lacking. These people cannot relax. They keep emotions under strict control. In their interpersonal relations, they are unduly conventional, serious, and formal.

Common characteristics of this personality style are orderliness, parsimoniousness, obstinacy, rigidity, and perseverance. Their perfectionism interferes with their ability to see "the big picture," preoccupied as they are with trivial details, rules, order, organization, schedules, and procedures. Their perceptive abilities seem to be restricted as they live in a world of regulations and hierarchies. They comply easily with the structures and rules set down by others. Although they may be perceived by others as industrious and efficient, they lack the flexibility and spontaneity that make for true effectiveness. In their meticulousness in going through daily routines they often get lost in detail.

These people insist that others submit to their way of doing things. Excessively judgmental and moralistic, both toward self and others, they lack awareness of the feelings elicited by their behavior. They see relationships in terms of dominance and submission, superiority and inferiority, and their behavior seems to be very much dependent on their position in the pecking order. They can be deferential, ingratiating, and even obsequious to superiors, while at the same time being autocratic and condemnatory to subordinates. To get their way, they often take recourse to rules and authorities higher than themselves. Their outlook has an authoritarian quality. These people demonstrate excessive devotion to work and productivity, to the exclusion of pleasure and enjoyment of interpersonal relationships. They are concerned with matters of organization and efficiency, constantly relating to others in terms of position in the pecking order.

Of course, what we are describing is the typical organization man, the person who accepts the correctness of the beliefs of the people in authority. The bureaucratic personality may be another name for such people, individuals who can function well both in superordinate and subordinate positions. But as with most things, the effectiveness of these people as leaders depends on a degree of balance between opposing forces. Some degree of control is necessary for the effective and efficient operating of an enterprise, but too much may inhibit creativity. A fairly successful mixture of styles often leading to leadership positions is a combination of the controlling and paranoid disposition, the first conducive to monitoring internal operations, the second useful to scan the outside environment. However, in the longer term, too much monitoring may become dysfunctional.

Control-oriented people can demonstrate a certain indecisiveness. Decision making is sometimes avoided or postponed, probably because of a nonspecific fear of making mistakes. Thus, procrastination may take over from action, raising questions about the controlling person's overall effectiveness. These types can become the Hamlets of organizations, not knowing what to do. Naturally, those exhibiting excessive indecisiveness are completely unsuitable for leadership positions.

THE PASSIVE-AGGRESSIVE PATTERN

David Post, the new president and CEO of Lotar, a highly diversified department store chain, was wondering what to do about Lawrence Neilson, one of his vice-presidents, a person who, like him, was relatively new on the job. David had become increasingly annoyed not only at Lawrence's way of running his department but also at his attitude toward David. Too many times meetings were canceled at the last moment; too many reports were left unfinished or were finished late in spite of promises to the contrary. Even worse, a number of projects were canceled halfway through for no good reason, greatly demotivating the people who had been working on them. David was also getting tired of hearing requests for deadline extensions. It just happened too often. He also thought that Lawrence seemed to be a master of passing the buck; somehow he always managed to avoid responsibility when something went wrong. But David had to hand it to him; he was really very good at finding excuses. It was always very hard to fault him. Whatever went wrong, there always seemed to be a plausible reason.

David felt, however, that one of these days he was not going to control himself any longer. He had had enough of it. That he hadn't blown his top yet was nothing short of a miracle. But then, there were always those second thoughts: how could he really? It was hard to get angry with someone who seemed so acquiescent. On the other hand, Lawrence never showed much enthusiasm for any assignment. Grumbling about it seemed to be more his style. Whatever the facts might be, David felt he could not stand much more of Lawrence's uncooperative, obstructionist behavior.

Out of curiosity, David had recently requested a careful check on Lawrence's background. And the report he had received was anything but laudatory. Lawrence's previous employers had revealed after some prompting that he had been fired from both of his jobs, the reason being that he didn't pay enough attention to detail and had made costly mistakes.

The example of Lawrence Neilson demonstrates that the characteristic that stands out among this group of people is resistance to demands for performance, both in occupational and social functioning. These people follow a strategy of negativism, defiance, and provocation. They are unable to make up their minds as to whether to adhere to the demands of others or to resist. Their behavior is characterized by both passivity and aggressiveness. They seem to be ambivalent about everything and cannot decide whether

77

to be dependent or independent, or whether to respond to events actively or passively. They struggle with the question of whether to give in or to assert themselves. They tend to express resistance indirectly through procrastination, dawdling, stubbornness, inefficiency, and forgetfulness. Their resistance often reflects hostility that they are afraid to show openly, but instead, have displaced. Covert aggression is a central feature. An aura of compliance and cordiality often masks negativistic resistance.

At the root of this behavior pattern probably lies a cognitive and emotional inability to assess clearly what is expected of one. We can hypothesize that in this respect these people are imitating their parents' frequent erratic, capricious, and conflicting demands, actions, and attitudes. It may be that during their upbringing they failed to learn what kind of behavior would pay off. External consistency and control may have been lacking. They often, therefore, seem to be fearful of commitments, unsure of their own desires, competences, and the reactions of others, and afraid to express feelings directly. Indecisiveness, contradictory behavior, and fluctuating attitudes become common patterns. These people shift rapidly and erratically from one type of behavior to the next, refusing to acknowledge their own responsibility for their difficulties.

Such people can be frequently irritable, sulky, moody, and unaccommodating, and can be very negative in their behavior. They have a tendency to complain, making everyone else's life miserable. Their disjointed, discontented self-image makes them feel misunderstood, cheated, and unappreciated in life. Consequently, they sometimes adopt the role of the martyr to indicate their distress.

An overriding characteristic of passive-aggressive people is pessimism toward the world, the belief that nothing ever works out for them. At the same time, they seem to be resentful and envious of the supposedly easy life of others. If things are going too well, they make sure they spoil it. By snatching defeat out of the jaws of victory, they recreate their expected disillusioning experiences.

Their unpredictable, conflicting, and vacillating behavior in social relationships frequently leads others to exasperation with them. Predictably, they constantly make enemies instead of friends, blaming others for shortcomings in accomplishments. They tend to make a mess out of interpersonal relationships. In spite of an often agreeable facade—they know that it is safer not to show hostility directly—they are basically unpleasant people to work for or with. Given their negativism and subtle defiance, their work history in organizations tends to be a checkered one. Underachievement due to self-destructive expressions of anger is common. Their ability to rise successfully in organizations may be questioned. Usually, their inability to engage in such basic activities as building alliances stifles their rise in organizations. Mixtures of this disposition with the histrionic, paranoid, or detached pattern does not fare much better in organizational life.

THE DEPENDENT DISPOSITION

Although Chris Simmons, chairman of the Medex Corporation, didn't mind people looking up to him and coming for advice and reassurance, he felt that there was a limit. What caused this reflection was the hard times he had dealing with Tom Kramer, his staff assistant. The latter seemed bright enough, able to write good reports, and had satisfactorily completed a number of complex special projects, but somehow something was missing.

No day went by without Tom coming to Chris's office, trying to see him to give him a progress report about his latest project and to ask him if it was satisfactory. Chris appreciated Tom's openness but felt that a person in Tom's position should be able to decide those things for himself. To have Tom recheck constantly with him about the correctness of his actions became too much of a demand on Chris's time. And whatever support he gave, it never seemed enough; Tom seemed to be insatiable. And after all, there were only so many hours in the day. Chris felt he had enough to do as it was.

Repeatedly, Chris had told Tom to figure things out for himself, to solve his own problems. But to no avail. Granted, he might have encouraged this type of behavior initially by telling Tom that he was a hands-on manager and wanted to be informed. But what Chris had got was more than he had bargained for. There was a difference between being informed and being a nursemaid. The question now was what to tell Tom about his future career prospects. Given his way of behaving, although he might do well in a staff position, to put Tom in a line job—the logical next career step—seemed risky.

This example demonstrates how people with this predisposition want others to assume responsibility for major areas of their lives because of their inability to function independently. These people seem to subordinate their own needs to those of others on whom they depend, to avoid the possibility of having to rely on themselves. They see themselves as powerless and prefer to play the inferior role, thereby denying their own individuality. In interpersonal relations they appear noncompetitive, self-effacing, even obsequious, ever-agreeable, compliant, and ingratiating. They lack assertiveness and avoid conflict. Their niceness, however, is partially a defense and may cover a considerable amount of hostility. Because of their excessive dependency needs and in order to avoid isolation and loneliness, they will submit themselves to being loyal no matter what the circumstances, and in spite of abuse and intimidation.

These people seem to lack self-confidence; their self-image is one of inadequacy. Their behavior has a helpless and hopeless quality. They suffer from self-doubt and wonder if they ever will be able to live up to others' expectations. They downgrade themselves, seeing themselves as ineffective, incompetent, or even stupid, claiming lack of abilities and virtues. In their search for support, given their hunger for social approval and affection, criticism becomes a devastating experience.

Dependent personalities lack initiative. They believe themselves to be at the mercy of events. Unable to assert themselves, they prefer a passive lifestyle, attaching themselves to others. They tend to abdicate responsibility. Instead, they search for an all-powerful, almost magical figure to take control. However, if they find a supportive partner, they may function surprisingly well. But even if that is the case, it is obvious that positions of leadership are not for them. Nor is leadership for people who show mixtures of styles that include this one: aspects of the histrionic, detached, masochistic, or controlling dispositions. Dependents don't have the degree of self-confidence and the spirit of competitiveness that it takes.

At the base of this behavior pattern usually lies parental overprotection. The inability of the parent to allow the child to go properly through the process of individuation stifles the development of the individual as a differentiated being. Thus, these children are not allowed to become less dependent and to satisfy their own wishes and fend for themselves. Contributing factors can be an overly anxious mother, the child's being the only one (behavior that may be accentuated due to illness of the child), or parents' fear of "losing the baby" with its obvious ramifications of aging and loneliness.

Another possible explanation for this disposition is that the person's dependency needs were highly frustrated because he or she was brought up in a family where there was not enough love to go around. Thus, we find here how a lack of love, and rejection instead of overconcern, by parents set the stage for a lifelong search to make up the deficit.

THE MASOCHISTIC DISPOSITION

Never I thought, would I make it through first grade; but I did, I even got a prize. I certainly won't pass the high-school entrance examinations; but pass I did. I'll definitely fail in my first year in high school; but no, I didn't fail, I succeeded in passing, time and time again.

Success, however, did not inspire confidence; on the contrary, I was always convinced . . . that the more I accomplished, the worse off I would be in the end. In my mind's eye I often saw a terrifying conclave of teachers

82

(the Gymnasium merely provides the most cogent example, but they were all around me) meeting to discuss this
unique, this absolutely outrageous case, to wit: how I, the
most incompetent, certainly the most ignorant of all, had
managed to sneak from first into the second gymnasium
grade, then into the third, and so on up the line. But now
that I had at last aroused their attention, I would of
course be immediately thrown out, to the immense
satisfaction of all righteous men delivered from a
nightmare.

This passage is taken from Kafka's famous *Letter to His
Father*. It gives a glimpse of his tendency to wallow in guilt
and his need for self-flagellation, or as he would write
himself, his "death wish." All through his actions and
writing we can find a strong streak of masochism. Suffering always stood central; life was a form of martyrdom. And
no one was more talented at extorting sympathy through
illness than Kafka.

As an employee of the Workmen's Accident Insurance
Institute, a position he held for sixteen years, he seems to
have been reasonably effective, although he himself viewed
his work as a way of killing time. His relationships with
his parents and women were another story altogether.
Wallowing in self-pity, he would never come to any decision, making great efforts to avoid happiness. Given his
outlook on life, his later discovery that he had tuberculosis
was almost welcomed by him as a form of salvation.

As the example of Franz Kafka illustrates, a considerable amount of similarity exists between this disposition and the dependent one. These dispositions often go
together. The difference is the discordant, self-defeating
quality of the behavior of people who fall into the maso-

83

chistic group. Self-devaluing and even self-damaging behavior is quite common. Here suffering stands central and
can be discerned by a frequent tendency to complain. Like
the dependent group, masochists are inclined to put themselves in an inferior position. They go out of their way to
prove themselves unlovable, to emphasize the worst features
of themselves, giving cause for acts of debasement. And by
relating to others in a self-sacrificing way, they encourage
and invite people to take advantage of them. They readily
accept blame for things for which they are not really
responsible, seemingly getting gratification from pain, suffering, and misfortune. Their emotional life is dramatic in
that it may quickly oscillate among feelings of love, rage,
and guilt toward themselves and others. Through provocation, they invite aggression, get angry themselves, and then
feel guilty afterward.

In deriving pleasure from exhibiting their misery,
masochists make "exhibitionism of ugliness" and "pride in
suffering" a way of life and a form of ingratiation. This way
of life may even take on a sexual dimension. These people
never really feel that they have lived up to the expectations
of others, and thus may engage in anticipatory self-
reproaches. In their inner world, no memories of achievement and success seem to exist. Instead, their inner imagery seems to be of debasement and devaluation. Among
these people we find the "criminals out of guilt," individuals
who commit criminal acts in the hope that some kind of
punishment will bring relief.

Ingratiation through sacrifice may result in masochists'
becoming the victims of unconsciously arranged accidents.
Symbolically, this can be viewed as a way of paying off their
guilt about being "bad," almost as if this were to be done

on an installment plan basis. Naturally, this tendency toward being accident-prone does not make for success in a leadership position. The self-depreciating quality of their behavior, their lack of self-confidence, their fear of or inhibitions about standing out, and their relatively passive modus operandi tends to leave masochists in a position of followership.

At the origin of this self-defeating constellation seems to be the child's desperate wish to arrive at some form of contact, whatever the price. The child may have learned that only "badness" gets a reaction from the parents. Some parents seem to offer only painful, unfulfilling contacts, and the child obliges. Apart from internalizing the badness, the child also internalizes the reproaching quality of the parent's behavior toward him or her, thus becoming his or her own worst enemy. Guilt about being angry at finding himself or herself in this situation and guilt about not living up to the expectations of the parents is part and parcel of this constellation.

HYBRIDS

Helene Fewings, the president of a faltering company in the apparel industry, seemed increasingly unwilling to face the declining profit position of her company. Even two months before the banks eventually took control, she held meetings during which she discussed nonexistent orders, the development of revolutionary new machinery, and the introduction of innovative products. These new developments were supposed to turn the company around and dramatically change its position in the industry. Fewings ignored the dismal profit-and-loss picture, inefficiencies in production, and poor sales performance, attributing them to unfair industry practices by competitors or even sabotage, and assured her managers that change was imminent and that the company would be out of the red shortly.

Sadly enough, these glorious ideas were far removed from reality. Adding to this unfortunate development was Fewing's increased isolation. Never having exactly been a "welcome wagon" before, she began to act even more detached as a result of the stress of the situation. It became more and more difficult to see her. Only those subordinates who agreed with her way of seeing things were able to approach her. Harbingers of bad news—meaning conflicting views—were not welcome. But even the sycophants had to be careful. Not much was needed to arouse her suspicions that they might be conspiring against her. The rare subordinate who questioned the beliefs of the president was looked at with contempt and would find himself or herself quickly out of a job. Only when the banks took control was the spell broken.

In this illustration we see an example of a mixture of styles. The CEO in question shows elements of the paranoid style in the ways she blames unfair practices by competitors or sabotage for her problems; at the same time, her increasing isolation is a symptom of the detached personality style. In fact, as illustrated earlier, hybrids, or mixtures of the styles, are more the rule than the exception, and the "normal" personality would recognize elements of many styles in his or her behavior. When trying to analyze one's own or a leader's personality, then, one should be very aware of this and should realize that the "pure" types I have described are fairly rare. Complicating the situation even more is the fact that differential diagnoses are all too often very difficult to make. An overview of the different personality styles (including the narcissistic one, which will be described in detail in Chapter 5) and the likelihood of finding each style in situations of leadership and followership is given in Table 1.

I have also indicated during the discussion that certain combinations gravitate toward leadership positions, while certain others tend toward followership. Certain mixtures of styles can at times be a winning combination, while other forms can be very dysfunctional, more susceptible to the F-dimension. As the exposé on narcissism in the next chapter will indicate, to possess elements of this particular style is often a sine qua non for leadership. For example, a combination of narcissism with control creates a kind of complementarity that can be very successful. In contrast, as can be learned from the preceding example, combining paranoia with detachment does not exactly make for effective leadership.

TABLE 1. An overview of the spectrum of personalities

Disposition	Likelihood of Leadership	Likelihood of Followership
Narcissistic	very high	low
Aggressive	high	low
Paranoid	high	medium
Histrionic	medium	high
Detached	medium	medium
Controlling	high	high
Passive-Aggressive	low	high
Dependent	very low	high
Masochistic	very low	high

And so we can arrive at many other leadership or followership combinations, effective or ineffective. For example, the clustering of dependence with masochism makes for very troubled followership. As mentioned earlier, the histrionic style, which by itself is found more often among followers, in combination with narcissism can make for very effective leadership. Moreover, although—as can be seen from the table—elements of certain styles are more likely to make for successful leadership than others, as in most instances, it is all a matter of degree. While moderation in mixtures of style may have no ill effect at all, excess, as always, will lead to ineffectiveness. And this question of excess brings us to the theme of narcissism.

5
Personal Glory
and Power:
Leadership in a
Narcissistic Age

It's a funny thing with psychopaths.
In normal times we render expert opinion on them,
in times of political unrest they rule us.
                                        Ernst Kretschmer

The situation in Iran and Libya exemplifies the timelessness of this statement made years ago by a German psychiatrist during Hitler's rise to power. The cases of Ayatollah Khomeini and Moammar Gadhafi dramatically illustrate the transforming power of leadership, placing in juxtaposition the forces of traditionalism and modernity. The developments in these countries are also good examples of the persistence of the regressive forces in humans that I have previously described and the easy arousal of passions by charismatic or messianic leaders. With great clarity they demonstrate our continuous search for guides or idols who can provide a vicarious sense of glory, prestige, and power, but who may also lead us to destruction.

The cultural historian Christopher Lasch has examined these aspects of contemporary leadership in what has been described as the "me decade" in his book *The Culture of Narcissism*. He strongly suggests that a new type of leadership is emerging due to the rise of narcissism. He argues that "narcissism appears realistically to represent the best way of coping with the tensions and anxieties of modern life, and the prevailing social conditions therefore tend to

91

bring out the narcissistic traits that are present, in varying degrees, in everyone.

Lasch does not stand alone. Comments about the rise of narcissism have come from many different sources. Mental health practitioners have expressed an increasing concern about people's retreat from public interests to a preoccupation with their own health and psyche, and about the upsurge of narcissistic personality disorders. And as I will explain, many people now see narcissism as the single most important personality style among those in positions of leadership.

THE EXCEPTIONS

With remarkable foresight, Sigmund Freud wrote early in this century about the various character types he met in clinical practice. One group he called "the Exceptions." He was referring to those people unwilling to submit to disagreeable necessity because of a special sense of entitlement. Such individuals believe that they have suffered enough; they should be spared future sacrifices. Moreover, they feel that they have the right to get back at their imagined tormentors. To illustrate this personality type, Freud quotes the opening soliloquy of Shakespeare's Richard III, who, having been born deformed, claims special privileges and argues that he has a right to be an exception, to disregard the scruples by which others let themselves be held back. He may do wrong himself, since wrong has been done to him. Richard III seems to be coping with feelings of worthlessness and low self-esteem the only way he knows, by letting go of his rage, of inner impotence, taking revenge, and in doing so, turning into a villain.

The search for personal glory and power coupled with vindictive action is an ageless phenomenon, and has often been regarded as the "disease" of kings, dictators, and prophets. In studying leaders we soon recognize that one critical component of their orientation is the quality and intensity of their narcissistic development. Freud, in his study of the relationship between leaders and followers, stated that "the leader himself need love no one else, he may be of a masterful nature, absolutely narcissistic, self-confident and independent." In his later writings, he introduced a narcissistic libidinal personality, an individual whose main interest is self-preservation, who is independent and impossible to intimidate. Significant aggressiveness is possible, which sometimes manifests itself in a constant readiness for activity. People belonging to this type impress others as strong personalities, as aggressive, independent, and action-oriented. According to Freud, in light of these characteristics, they are ideally suited for leadership.

This intruding preoccupation with the self, however, is not the exclusive domain of the more dramatic charismatic and messianic leaders. We can argue that narcissistic behavior has become truly democratized, and is now part and parcel of everyday life. Some students of this phenomenon even go so far as to say that in modern society the narcissistic personality has become the backbone of organizational life and leadership. For example, Lasch contends that the narcissist "rises to positions of prominence not only in awareness movements and other cults but in busi-

93

ness corporations, political organizations, and government bureaucracies. For all his inner suffering, the narcissist has many traits that make for success in bureaucratic institutions, which put a premium on the manipulation of interpersonal relations, discourage the formation of deep personal attachments, and at the same time provide the narcissist with the approval he needs in order to validate his self-esteem. . . . The management of personal impressions comes naturally to him, and his mastery of its intricacies serves him well in political business organizations where performance now counts for less than 'visibility,' 'momentum,' and a winning record. As the 'organizational man' gives way to the bureaucratic 'gamesman'—the 'loyalty era' of American business to the age of the 'executive success game'—the narcissist comes into his own."

To take an example from the business world: It had always looked as if Jim Munro was going to be successful in whatever endeavor he undertook. And until recently he had certainly been doing very well. But now things had begun to fall apart, and lately, he had been spending more and more time thinking about his problems. Earlier, he had always felt reluctant to give these matters much thought. Granted, he had been upset before. He had never been a stranger to anger and resentment when something did not go his way, and he certainly did have his bad moods. But now, it seemed somehow different. Feelings of restlessness, futility, and dissatisfaction had begun to bother him. He could no longer rationalize nor dismiss them.

Of course, there was the question of his work. Not much seemed to be happening at the moment; in fact, things seemed to be stagnating. No longer did he have a sense of exhilaration, the feeling that everything was possible.

Instead, he now felt let down, empty, and he sometimes even experienced a sense of being not quite real. He felt he was not going anywhere any longer.

What had really started this whole process of introspection had been the sudden unexpected departure of his wife. He still did not quite understand why she had left. She had told him she felt they didn't have a meaningful relationship. Sure enough, he had never felt that close to her, but it had been nice to have her around. He had always given her what she wanted. As far as he could tell there was really no reason for her to have left. Now he felt resentful, cheated. Why had he never been given a warning signal that something was wrong? Why hadn't she told him? She had always seemed full of admiration for him, and then suddenly this bombshell. But that was not all; other things were also upsetting him. Lately he had become concerned about his physical condition. He often felt tired and occasionally had pains in his back. Sometimes he wondered if he was not suffering from some mysterious, incurable disease.

The more he thought about it, the more he realized that he had always felt special. And true enough, most of his life he had managed to be in the limelight, the center of praise and admiration. This had been the case as long as he could remember. Certainly, his good looks had helped. But it was more than that; he did have talents. He could still vividly remember how his parents would ask him to play popular tunes on the piano at their parties when he was a kid. Did they applaud and cheer! But in spite of all the attention, somehow it had never seemed quite enough for him.

Most of the people who met Jim felt that he had great promise. He did have his doubts sometimes, but that was a fleeting feeling that he would quickly push aside. He remembered with great satisfaction how he had been listed in his high school yearbook at graduation as the person most likely to succeed. And why not—he had been extremely popular!

After graduating from an MBA program at a well-known eastern business school, he had found it difficult to choose among the many job offers that came his way. He had been one of the most successful job interviewees. He remembered how easy it had been to charm the recruiters. And given his interest in the media, advertising had been the logical choice. He had always liked glamorous things. All who knew him felt he had embarked on a brilliant career. He recalled how contagious his enthusiasm and self-assuredness had been in the firm. It sure had helped, and explained the succession of rapid promotions. But what had gone wrong?

Those who were closely associated with Jim Munro acquired over time very mixed feelings about him. Sure enough, initially they had all been taken in by his personality, but gradually, greater exposure to his behavior had made them wonder. Questions about him were being raised from many directions.

His subordinates had come to recognize some of the darker sides of his personality. Relationships with Jim always seemed to be lopsided. He tended to take other people's admiration about his work for granted. He never seemed to have time, however, to pay any attention to their needs. They recalled that managers unwilling to show enthusiasm for his ideas could quickly find themselves out of his favor. His high sense of self-worth was sometimes hard to take. Furthermore, arousing his envy could be quite dangerous. They remembered occasions where he had gone out of his way to put rivals in a bad light, and he could be very arrogant and vindictive. It had become very clear to them how little was needed for someone to fall from grace.

His superiors, although initially taken by his charm and apparent talents, also had second thoughts about him. They had noticed how callous he could be in appraising his subordinates. Dealing with him seemed always very smooth—but somehow too smooth. When they really gave it some thought they had to admit that relating to him left them with an empty feeling afterward. There never seemed to be any depth in the interchange. And that lack of depth was also reflected in his work. It had taken a long time to determine what was really wrong. But now they realized how superficial most of his activities had really been. Goals were never completely met; somehow, something was always missing. The original great promise was never fulfilled.

The person I have been describing is of course the narcissist, an individual who is, as I have said, very common in modern organizations. The narcissistic executive is usually heralded as a person possessing great potential; but over time it becomes clear that something is lacking. Things do not seem to work out. Although many of these individuals can be extremely effective executives, frequently their original promise is never really fulfilled. Eventually, problems arise. Not only does their incessant need for admiration and the exploitative nature of their relationships cause irritation, but also their performance at work never seems to be completely right. There is a gamesmanlike quality about their behavior. In their striving for success, they readily manipulate others, excelling in power games. Unfortunately, the persons themselves are often not really aware of why they are behaving the way they do. Usually, only the onset of physical aging, career setbacks, marital problems, and the increasing experience of the emptiness in their relationships makes them begin to wonder what is happening to them.

WHAT IS NARCISSISM?

Narcissism has two faces, like Janus. Some self-love is required for survival: without concern for the self, the organism dies. On the other hand, too great a preoccupation with the self can become self-destructive. To understand how this balance is achieved and what happens when it is upset, we have to look back to experiences in early childhood.

A child's sense of identity is only gradually acquired, through interactions with the environment. For normal character development, the child has to be able to push against constraining forces, and a necessary part of this process is encountering a certain degree of frustration. The intensity of frustration, however, varies. Researchers of child development have argued that what makes for normal development is age-appropriate frustration without traumatization. The developing child, as a way of coping with the shortcomings of parental care and in an attempt to ward off frustration, likes to retain the original experience of perfection and bliss of his early years by creating both an all-powerful, grandiose, exhibitionistic image of the self, and an all-powerful idealized image of the parent, the latter taking on the role of savior and protector. These two narcissistic configurations can be called the grandiose self and the idealized parent image, and as we have seen in Chapter 3 can be revived as transference reactions.

In normal circumstances the grandiosity and exhibitionism of this grandiose self are gradually tamed by the forces of reality. Originally, these activities are seen as through a mirror, a process whereby the parents reflect and participate in the grandiosity of the child, confirming the latter's self-esteem. Eventually, the parents modify this exhibitionistic display, channeling grandiose fantasies about power and glory in a realistic direction. A basis is formed for well-grounded ambition, directed activities, and a secure sense of self-esteem.

The same can be said about the idealized parent image. While initially in the developmental process complete union is needed with the admired, omnipotent figure to prevent a sense of depletion and helplessness, in normal situations the child's evaluation of the other person becomes increasingly realistic. The child begins to internalize these more realistic elements of the other as part of his or her permanent personality structure, eventually using these elements as guides for ideals and ambitions.

Over time, most people develop relatively stable ways of representing the experiences of themselves and others. These psychic representations in one's private inner world are known as internal objects. They are composed of pleasurable and painful experiences, fantasies, ideals, thoughts, and images that help to create a cognitive and affective map of the world. In creating this map the developing child has to resolve the relationship between real, external people and the mental images retained of these people. Thus, our interactions with actual people depend not only on how we view them, but also on our views of internal others. These psychic representations profoundly influence our affective and cognitive states as well as our behavior and actions. Good internal objects have a generative and restorative function, and serve as a source of sustenance in dealing with life's adversities. They constitute the underpinnings of healthy functioning. But in the absence of good internal objects, various dysfunctions can occur. Therein lies the genesis of pathological behavior. Naturally, the earliest objects are the parents whose nurturing gives rise to different kinds of internal worlds. Since parents are not always consistent in dealing with their children, this world can be highly confusing and turbulent.

In some situations, then, prolonged disappointments due to parental understimulation, overstimulation, or nonintegrative, inconsistent interventions during this vulnerable early period of development can lead to problems. Looking at these cases we notice that at a superficial level many of these parents seem to treat their children well. Closer observation, however, may show a completely different picture, and we can discern how callous and indifferent their treatment really is. Frequently, such parents use their children as an extension of themselves in their own search for admiration and greatness. Facilitating this form of exploitation is the fact that many of these children often possess real qualities that may cause admiration, such as physical attractiveness or special talents, attributes that may fit the parents' purposes. Such admiration, however, unfortunately only creates the illusion of being loved without really taking the needs of the children into consideration. When parents use their children as a way of compensating for their own disappointments, the search for admiration by the children may become a lifelong endeavor to offset their feelings of just being used, not being loved for themselves. Thus self-love can actually be viewed as a cover for self-hatred. In these instances, both the grandiose self and the idealized parent images are not really modified and truly integrated, but continue to exist in their unaltered forms, pursuing their archaic aims. A cohesive sense of self is absent, leading to an imbalance in psychic structure, incoherent behavior, and problems in self-esteem regulation.

Thus, a narcissist like Jim Munro looks at the world as a mirror, reflecting what he likes to see, continually in search of an admiring audience to support his need for grandiosity and combat his feelings of helplessness. It is a world of instant gratification, where desires are never really met and where rage retains a primitive quality.

Although the narcissistic type of personality has long been recognized, only relatively recently has it come under critical scrutiny. For example, the latest version of *DSM III* lists the following criteria to describe narcissistic personality disorders:

> A pervasive pattern of grandiosity (in fantasy or behavior), lack of empathy, and hypersensitivity to the evaluation of others, beginning by early adulthood and present in a variety of contexts, as indicated by at least *five* of the following:
>
> 1) reacts to criticism with feelings of rage, shame, or humiliation (even if not expressed);
> 2) is interpersonally exploitative: takes advantage of others to achieve his or her own ends;
> 3) has a grandiose sense of self-importance, e.g., exaggerates achievements and talents, expects to be noticed as "special" without appropriate achievement;

4) believes that his or her problems are unique and can be understood only by other special people;

5) is preoccupied with fantasies of unlimited success, power, brilliance, beauty, or ideal love;

6) has a sense of entitlement: unreasonable expectation of especially favorable treatment, e.g., assumes that he or she does not have to wait in line when others must do so;

7) requires constant attention and admiration, e.g., keeps fishing for compliments;

8) lack of empathy: inability to recognize and experience how others feel, e.g., annoyance and surprise when a friend who is seriously ill cancels a date;

9) is preoccupied with feelings of envy.

In this description we find overtones of mental illness and serious impairment of functioning. Many of these characteristics, however, are also applicable, albeit in smaller measure, to narcissistic individuals who adopt a more "normal" mode of functioning.

We can see, then, how narcissists feel they must rely on themselves rather than on others for the gratification of life's needs. They live with the assumption that they cannot reliably depend on anyone's love or loyalty. They pretend to be self-sufficient, but in the depth of their being they experience a sense of deprivation and emptiness. To cope with these feelings and, perhaps, as a cover for their insecurity, narcissistic individuals become preoccupied with establishing their usefulness, power, beauty, status, prestige, and superiority. At the same time, narcissists expect others to accept the high esteem in which they like to hold themselves, and to cater to their needs. Thus, the factor that becomes striking in the behavior of these people is their interpersonal exploitativeness. Narcissistic individuals live under the illusion that they are entitled to be served, that their own desires take precedence over those of others. They think that they deserve special consideration in life.

It must be emphasized, however, that these characteristics occur with different degrees of intensity. A certain dose of narcissism is necessary to function effectively. We all show signs of narcissistic behavior. And among individuals who possess only modest narcissistic tendencies, we find those who are very talented and capable of making great contributions to society. Those who gravitate toward the extremes, however, give narcissism its perjorative reputation. Here we find excesses of rigidity, narrowness, resistance, vindictiveness, and discomfort in dealing with the external environment.

VARIETIES OF NARCISSISTIC EXPERIENCE

Given their need for power, prestige, and glamour, it is to be expected that many narcissistic personalities eventually end up in leadership positions. Their ability to manipulate others and their capacity to establish quick, superficial relationships serve them well in organizational life. And they can be quite successful, particularly in areas that allow them to fulfill their ambitions of greatness, fame, and glory. Unfortunately, in many instances, power and prestige tend to be more important to these people than commitment to goals and performance. Their primary concern usually remains the preservation of their own greatness and specialness with a contemptuous disregard of others.

Leaders can be said to occupy different positions on a spectrum ranging from healthy narcissism to pathology. The categories we are dealing with are by no means distinct. The factors that distinguish between health and dysfunction are the intrapsychic and interpersonal dynamics of the leader.

Reactive Narcissism

In describing messianic and charismatic leaders, the psychoanalyst Heinz Kohut, a major contributor to the study of narcissism, argues that such leaders suffer from a pathology of narcissistic development. The two important spheres of the self—which, as we have seen, are built upon our tendency to obtain reassurance through mirroring (the grandiose self) and our tendency to feel more powerful through identification (the idealized parental image)—are poorly integrated in this type of narcissist. Phase-appropriate development in their early years did not occur. Frustrating experiences were poorly handled. As children, they acquired instead a defective, not well-integrated sense of identity and subsequently were unable to maintain a stable sense of self-esteem. To cope with such feelings, these individuals created for themselves a self-image of specialness. This can be viewed as a compensatory, reactive refuge against an ever-present feeling of never having been loved by their parents. The internal world of such people is very likely to be populated by malevolent images. In some way or another they are trying to cope with this disturbing imagery.

Naturally, to create an illusion of uniqueness is one way of coping, but one that has a glass bubble quality. This

104

inner fragility vitally affects the individual's dealings with the external environment. Any discrepancies between capacities and wants are likely to accentuate anxiety and impair reality testing; the person becomes unable to distinguish wish from perception or, to put it another way, "inside" from "outside." Individuals with this reactive orientation frequently distort outside events to manage anxiety and to prevent a sense of loss and disappointment. As extreme examples in the political sphere we can list people such as Hitler, Stalin, and Mussolini.

If such people are in a position of leadership this can have grave consequences. These leaders tend to gravitate toward followers who are sycophants. They don't like to receive information that runs counter to their scheme of things. Also, a strong Machiavellian streak may run through their behavior. They couldn't care less about hurting others in pursuit of their own interests. And their need to devalue others to underline their own superiority can have serious consequences. Empathy seems to be completely lacking. Projects are undertaken on a grand scale but are often doomed to fail because of lack of judgment and an absence of reality testing. Of course, if things go wrong, the narcissist blames others.

Self-Deceptive Narcissism

We often find a second type of narcissistic leader with a very different pattern of early childhood development. Such self-deceptive leaders probably have been overstimulated or overburdened. Like Jim Munro in our earlier example, these individuals were once led by one or both parents to believe that they were completely lovable and perfect,

105

regardless of their actions and in spite of reality. Such children become the proxies of their parents, entrusted with a mission to fulfill many unrealized parental hopes. They are anxious because of the ideals of perfection given to them by their parents. Deep down they wonder if they can live up to these ideals. We notice that what may appear as indulgence on the part of the parents is, in fact, exactly the opposite. The parents use their children to take care of their own needs, overburdening them with their implicit desires. When parents impose their unrealistic hopes on their children, they create delusions. They confuse the children about their true abilities.

Such unrealistic beliefs may sometimes be the original impetus that differentiates these individuals from others and makes them successful. Perhaps Freud had this in mind when he noted that "if a man has been his mother's un-disputed darling, he retains throughout life the triumphant feeling, the confidence in success, which not seldom brings actual success along with it." In those instances when such early encouragement works out, the child may be sufficiently talented to live up to the parents' exaggerated expectations. A person who in more normal circumstances might have led an ordinary life may use the expectations imposed on him or her as a child as a basis for excellence.

In general, however, the self-delusory quality of the unrealistic beliefs created by parents leads to problems. An exalted self-image is usually difficult to sustain in the light of external circumstances such as disappointment and failure. Thus, even though the images in such children's inner theater are benign, disturbing interpersonal encounters when they venture forth from the protective family environment will give them an element of instability or frailty. The overvalued image of the self that was garnered from an idealizing parent becomes more realistic after interactions with more honest and critical peers. Still, the traumas of early disappointments may leave a somewhat fragile and distorted concept of self. Self-deceiving narcissists are likely to suffer from interpersonal difficulties due to their desire to live up to the now-internalized parental illusions of self-worth. They tend to demonstrate emotional superficiality and poverty of affection. Their behavior has an ideal-hungry quality: they are looking for others to provide structure to their lives, a result of difficulties in identity formation.

Self-deceptive narcissistic leaders are much more approachable than their reactive counterparts. They are not nearly as exploitative and are more tolerant of dissenting opinions. They also appear more insecure. They are wary of threats in the environment and want to avoid making mistakes. They are therefore more conservative in their approach than the reactive group, having a more analytical orientation. Self-deceptive narcissistic leaders are not as quick to devalue others, are more eager to please, and are willing to engage in deals and exchanges with their followers. Their leadership style has more of a transactional quality as opposed to the reactive leaders who are more concerned with how to transform their followers, preoccupied as the latter are with furthering their more grandiose needs.

Thus, conceptually, we can differentiate between reactive and self-deceptive narcissism. In practice, however, a distinction is more difficult to make. Parents might each have responded differently toward the developing child. One parent might have taken a cold, hostile, rejecting attitude,

107

while the other might have been supportive. Thus could have been created different gradations of benign and malevolent internal objects, which accounts for mixtures of narcissistic styles. In addition, instead of being frustrated when ambitious parental expectations are incongruent with external reality, children can sometimes strive successfully to bring their abilities up to their perceived capacity, as Freud notes. Moreover, as we have pointed out, learning experiences later in life may also have buffering or mitigating effects.

Constructive Narcissism

Constructive narcissists do not behave in a reactive or self-deceptive manner. They do not feel the same need to distort reality to deal with life's frustrations. Nor are they so prone to anxiety. They make less frequent use of primitive defenses, such as splitting, projection, and idealization, and are less estranged from their feelings, wishes, and thoughts. In fact, they often generate a sense of positive vitality that derives from confidence about their personal worth. Their inner theater is populated with benign imagery, which sustains them in the face of life's adversities. They are willing to express their wants and to stand behind their actions, regardless of the reactions of others. They have a strong sense of self-confidence based on encouragement by their parents. Independence of thought has been encouraged while growing up. Moreover, they were helped by their parents to see things in perspective and to avoid scapegoating and other destructive activities. Most important, their parents did not overburden them but kept their expectations in balance, permitting accurate reality testing. When

108

disappointed, such people do not act spitefully, but are ready to uplift others and engage in reparative action. That is, they have the patience to wait for the moment when their talents will be needed. Boldness in action, introspection, and thoughtfulness are common. In the political domain, leaders such as Nehru and John F. Kennedy are good illustrations. Prime examples from corporate life are people like Carlo De Benedetti and Richard Branson.

These leaders are no strangers to manipulation and not beyond the occasional act of opportunism. But they are generally able to get on fairly well with their subordinates, having developed a relationship of give and take. Constructive narcissists possess a high degree of confidence in their abilities and are highly task- and goal-oriented. They are willing to take ultimate responsibility for their decisions, not blaming others when things go wrong. They may sometimes come across as lacking in warmth and consideration, substituting reciprocity in relationships with abstract concerns such as "the good of the company" or "the welfare of all." Their sense of inner direction, however, gives them the ability to inspire others and create a common cause, transcending petty self-interests. It gives their leadership style both a transactional and transforming quality.

In summary, reactive narcissists tend to be ruthless, grandiose, and exhibitionistic. They show a desire to dominate and control and are extremely exploitative. Self-deceptive narcissists are milder: they want to be liked and are much less tyrannical. Still, they lack empathy, are obsessed mainly with their own needs, and are given to being discreetly Machiavellian. Their behavior has an "as if" quality, because they lack a strong sense of inner conviction and identity. Finally, constructive narcissistic leaders are also quite ambitious and can be manipulative and hypersensitive to criticism. But they have enough self-confidence, adaptability, and humor to stress real achievements. They get on well with others because of their insights into relationships.

STRENGTHS AND WEAKNESSES

As I have said, a certain degree of narcissistic behavior is essential for leadership success, and narcissism can in some cases be a strength in a leader. We have seen that leadership necessitates some degree of callousness, a quality needed to be sufficiently independent from others to be able to make what can be at times very difficult decisions. This attitude of independence can have a healthy protective function in that it serves as a buffer against regressive interpersonal and group pressures. As with most things, it is all a matter of degree. A moderate dose of grandiosity and idealization transformed into self-confidence about one's capabilities and expressed in the ability to identify with senior executives and the organization (as is exemplified by the constructive narcissistic leader) contributes to effective organizational functioning. In such instances, the excitement generated by the narcissistic leader can have a great positive impact. The radiation of self-confidence and purposefulness can be extremely contagious.

Obviously, such leadership behavior becomes particularly effective for organizations in crisis, where enthusiasm and purpose are needed to create motivation and momentum. In a faltering organization it may create the long-needed desire for goal-directedness and group cohesion. It can create a greater alertness to internal and external danger signs. These are the times when the word *charismatic* is heard. An excessive dose of such behavior, however, can lead to psychological impairment and destructiveness. At what point constructive forces turn into destructive ones depends on the situation. To determine the turning point is not always an easy matter.

Unfortunately, the sense of excitement generated by narcissistic leaders tends to be temporary; it easily wears off. The other side of narcissistic leadership behavior may be shown. The lack of conviction that characterizes so many of these leaders, and their tendency to resort to political expediency at the cost of long-term goals may become apparent. Action that originally was interpreted as bold and imaginative may become viewed as opportunism. Moreover, such leaders' inability to accept a real interchange of ideas and the self-righteousness that many of them exhibit may impair organizational functioning and prevent organizational adaptation to internal and external changes. Their lack of genuine problem solving, their intolerance for positive criticism, and their inability to compromise can inevitably have serious negative effects. When this happens, the F-dimension has become operative.

One of the important roles of a leader is to cater to the emotional needs of his or her subordinates. Leaders pushed by the forces of excessive narcissism seem unable to do this. They disregard their subordinates' legitimate dependency needs, and instead take advantage of the loyalty of the people dependent on them. They behave callously, are overcom-

111

petitive, and resort to an excessive use of deprecation. This behavior fosters submissiveness and passive dependency, thus stifling the critical functions of their managers. Their lack of commitment to others, discarding their subordinates when they are no longer needed for their purposes, and their search for new alliances do not foster a creative organizational culture.

POSSIBLE INTERVENTIONS

As indicated, constructive narcissistic leaders pose few organizational problems. But what can other executives do about the two more dysfunctional types of leaders? In situations where the organization is centralized and the narcissistic leader is dominant, poor performance and subsequent dismissal by a strong board of directors may be the only effective catalysts for change. And even these mutative influences are ruled out when a leader has a significant shareholder position and no other party is a major shareholder.

It is very difficult to change a narcissist's personality. If such a person becomes dysfunctional there is often no other remedy than to transfer him or her out of harm's way or to reduce his or her influence. A number of structural devices can be used to accomplish the latter. For example, power can be more broadly distributed in the organization so that many people get involved in strategic decisions and lower-level managers are induced to take responsibility for more routine concerns. Cross-functional committees, task forces, parallel structures, and executive committees can provide forums in which other managers can express their

112

viewpoints, providing opportunities for the narcissistic leader to learn from and have his or her influence mitigated by others. Monolithic and unrealistic perspectives are thereby discouraged. Moreover, trying to identify excessive narcissism in recruitment and making promotions is a form of preventive maintenance.

When all these possible interventions fail and the narcissistic behavior of a leader becomes extreme, outside professional help is needed, if the individual is willing to consider that alternative. The pain that accompanies many of these narcissistic behavior patterns is usually the driving force. The usual sign that a general receptivity to change may exist is the manifestation of certain stress symptoms. In such instances the leader finally may realize that something is wrong. What is wrong tends to be not very specific but may center around vague complaints about dissatisfaction with life, feelings of futility, lack of purpose, and even a sense of being fraudulent. Sometimes comments can be heard about the absence of meaningful relationships, lack of excitement in work, and the ability only to resort to routines. Mood swings, depression following excitement and rage, and hypochondriacal concerns may come to the fore. In general, as could be seen in the example of Jim Munro, a pervasive sense of inner emptiness is noted.

Recognition of what these complaints represent is important. It is the cornerstone on which the individual and the concerned parties can build their change effort. The task becomes to expand the capacity to care for others without the fear of rejection and humiliation. This implies the establishment of a more secure sense of self-esteem and the lessening of the need for grandiosity and idealization.

113

through the establishment of more benign inner images. The bolstering of a fragile sense of self eventually creates a greater cohesiveness of inner imagery: internalized images lose their archaic malevolent content and become more in tune with outer reality. A secure sense of self-esteem also tames feelings of inner rage and envy of others and makes for conviction, purpose, and creativity. Relationships of trust become the building blocks for the development of empathy, creativity, humor, and wisdom, forming a base for effective leadership. If narcissistic behavior can be channeled in these directions, narcissism can be the motor that drives any organization.

6
Folie à Deux: Leaders Driving Their Followers Mad

So this is hell. I'd never have believed it.
You remember all we were told about the torture chambers,
the fire and brimstone, the "burning marl." Old wives' tales!
There's no need for red-hot pokers. Hell is—other people!

Jean-Paul Sartre, *No Exit*

An understanding of the various personality styles I have described in the previous two chapters will help us make sense out of what would otherwise be described as just the personality quirks of leaders. But we must go further than this. We must be aware that these styles may also affect others who come into contact with leaders, making others, too, behave in an apparently irrational way. In fact, dysfunction in the CEO can produce ripples throughout an entire organization. The behavior of J. Edgar Hoover, once in charge of the FBI, is a good example. Hoover struck many as an erratic autocrat, banishing agents to obscure posts for the most whimsical reasons and terrorizing them with so many rules and regulations that adherence to all of them would have been an impossibility. Hoover viewed his directorship of the FBI as infallible; subordinates soon learned that dissent equaled disloyalty. No whim of Hoover's was considered too insignificant to be ignored. For example, refusal to participate in an anti-obesity program was likely to incur his wrath, and rumor had it that chauffeurs had to avoid making left turns while driving him (apparently his car had once been hit by another car when he was making a left turn).

If it originated with Hoover, a trivial and unimportant order changed in meaning. Even if the directive was unclear, subordinates would have to take some form of calculated action and, it was said, should expect trouble if they did not take the directive seriously. Nurtured by those in the organization who followed them, these directives often assumed a life of their own. Only appearances of and actual slavish obedience to the rules, and statistical accomplishments such as increasing the monetary value of fines levied or the number of criminals convicted or fugitives apprehended, counted. And problems arose if the figures did not increase each year.

Naturally, those agents who embraced the concept of the director's omnipotence were more likely to succeed. To ensure compliance, inspectors would be sent out to field offices in search of violations (the breaking of some obscure rule or instruction). If a "contract was out" on the special agent in charge of the office, a "violation" would inevitably be found. Apparently, the inspector's own future at the FBI was at stake if no violations were discovered because then, in turn, a contract might be issued on him or her. If one wanted to survive in the organization, participation in many of these absurdities was often unavoidable. Many of these bizarre activities seem to have been treated as quite normal aspects of organizational life and were carried out with great conviction.

While Hoover at the FBI, Hitler in the bunker just before the collapse of the Third Reich, and, more recently, Jim Jones at the mass suicide in Guyana are newsworthy examples of what leaders can do to their subordinates when

118

they lose touch with reality, the effects of certain personality quirks also occur in less heralded tales and in a business context.

What is striking about the anecdote of Hoover is the shift of delusions and unusual behavior patterns from the originator of the activities to one or more others who were closely associated with him. These associates not only took an active part but also frequently enhanced and elaborated on these delusions. And the delusions seemed to escalate in intensity when the people involved tried to solve problems concerned. They inevitably aggravated the situation, made it worse, and became correspondingly more and more reluctant to face external reality. Feeling most comfortable in their own chosen, closed environment, they did not welcome the opinion of outsiders, seeing them as threatening the status quo and disturbing their tunnel vision.

Also noticeable in this example is just how contagious the behavior of a leader can be, and how devastating its effect on followers and organization. In Hoover's case, the reaction of his subordinates further encouraged him to continue in his dysfunctional behavior. Perhaps the particular mission of Hoover's organization may have contributed to the fact that very few subordinates were willing to refuse to participate in some of these bizarre activities. Whatever the reason, many conformed to his wishes and some may actually have believed in the appropriateness and importance of his actions. We have here an example of transferential tendencies and can see the predominance of the paranoid and dependent style, and how these styles can complement each other.

In psychoanalytic and psychiatric literature, mental contagion—or, in other words, the way one person can drive

119

another person crazy—has been a recurring theme. This particular process of influence, which usually goes together with some form of break with reality occurring among groups of individuals, is generally known as folie à deux— that is, shared madness.

THE DYNAMICS OF FOLIE À DEUX

Two French psychiatrists were the first to coin the term *folie à deux*. Other names given to this phenomenon have been *double insanity, mental contagion, collective insanity,* or *psychosis of association.* Folie à deux essentially involves the sharing of a delusional system by two or more individuals. Usually, this phenomenon has been studied among family members living an isolated existence. This does not mean, however, that it cannot occur in other situations such as business or politics.

To better understand this psychological process, let us turn once more to early childhood development. Closer investigation reveals that one central theme in the origin of this disorder appears to be the degree of success or failure its instigator has had in establishing feelings of basic trust with people (originally with the parents). As we have seen in discussing the paranoid style, intrusiveness and overcontrol by others can contribute to a lack of cohesive sense of self, a sense of betrayal, and a perception of the environment as hostile and dangerous. The individual's personality will develop accordingly.

Hence, in dealings with others, such a person will continually take precautions and be on guard to be ready for any confirmation of suspicions. In situations of power, as a reactive way of dealing with what he or she sees as

a hostile environment, the individual will be highly susceptible to grandiose fantasies and prone to delusions.

Apart from suffering from this emerging paranoid disposition, a person who lacks trust also suffers an absence
of closeness and, consequently, may have seriously frustrated dependency needs. For such a person, the world becomes a dangerous place where only a few individuals can
be trusted. If an opportunity arises to satisfy these dependency needs, the attachment this person makes to others
can become extremely intense, frequently overpowering all
other behavior patterns. Because this person's attachment
is so important, he or she will do anything—even sacrifice
reality—to preserve it.

Individuals to whom this attachment is directed, and
who are not without their own dependency needs (though
perhaps these are not of such an intense nature), may enjoy the way the other person is taking care of them and
giving them some form of direction and guidance in life.
One outcome may be that they will *strongly identify* with
those things for which the other person stands. However,
the price for these feelings of closeness becomes the *uncritical* acceptance of the behavior and actions of the
domineering person, often without much concern for its
base in reality. This identification process appears to be
of a special nature, and contains elements of the earlier
described defense mechanism called identification with the
aggressor.

One may gain insight into what is frequently described
as an eccentric leadership style if one studies emotionally
charged leader-follower relationships, characterized by
some kind of impaired ability to see things realistically,
within the context of folie à deux. One may discover that

121

this phenomenon, with various degrees of intensity, is a regular occurrence in organizations and can be considered one of the risks of leadership.

Leaders should not underestimate the degree of influence they wield in their organizations. Idealizing transference patterns are always operative. Recognizing dependency—the need for direction—as one of our most universal characteristics, leaders should be aware that many of their subordinates will sacrifice reality for its sake, participating in even irrational decisions without mustering a critical stand and challenging what is happening.

To preserve this dependency relationship, both leaders and followers may create closed communities, losing touch with the immediate reality of the organization's environment to the detriment of organizational functioning. When the reality is not abandoned completely, however, this phenomenon is often difficult to recognize. But in view of its damaging consequences in organizations, even in a limited form, it deserves serious attention.

DEFECTIVE REALITY TESTING IN ORGANIZATIONS

Suppose a senior executive under the strain of leadership, trying to cope with often disconcerting imagery of power and control in addition to the general pressures of the business environment, gradually loses touch with the organization's reality. This individual's charismatic personality may once have attracted executives with highly ungratified dependency needs to the organization, people who were prone to fall into an idealizing pattern. Or it may

have been the organizational culture itself that was conducive to a reawakening of these executives' dependency
needs and idealizing transference patterns.

Whatever the reason, during their association with the
organization these managers may have become dependent
on their leader. Although strong, these needs do not at first
completely overpower all other behavior patterns. What,
however, changes the dependent disposition into folie à
deux? When does such a relationship assume dysfunctional
characteristics? When both leader and subordinates become dependent on each other in a situation that offers few
outside sources of gratification, their complete commitment to each other can be taken as symptomatic.

At some point, triggered by an event usually associated
with a depriving experience of the past, some leaders may
become preoccupied with delusionary ideas (and this is not
necessarily a conscious process), one of them being that
their subordinates are taking unfair advantage of them.
This may arouse a certain amount of anger. But, at the same
time, since the subordinates' expressions of attachment
finally fulfill the leader's own dependency needs that have
been ungratified for so long, such a leader is very ambivalent and feels guilty about this feeling of hostility.

In spite of lingering resentment, therefore, such leaders
are extremely reluctant to give up their relationships with
their subordinates. These may be among the few close relationships they have been able to establish. Consequently,
to defend themselves against their own emerging hostility
toward their subordinates, some leaders will externalize
and attribute this hostility to others.

Such a leader absolves closely associated executives of
responsibility for these feelings; it is "the others" who are

to blame. This blame can take many forms, eventually encapsulating everything that may be going wrong with the company. The leader, who has been the originator of this process, now needs his or her subordinates to support these delusionary ideas and actions. Leaders need that support not only because the ideas are their defense against hostility but also because they may lose these feelings of closeness with their subordinates if they do not get it. There seems to be only one option—namely, to induce their subordinates to participate.

If a subordinate resists, such leaders become overtly hostile, including them in their vision of "the other camp"—the enemy. Naturally, the subordinate's level of anxiety rises. A double-bind situation develops for the subordinate; he or she has to choose between the loss of gratification of his or her dependency needs and exposure to the wrath of the leader, on the one hand, and the loss of reality, on the other.

In many instances, subordinates solve this intrapsychic conflict by giving in to the psychological ultimatum to identify with the aggressor. They thus satisfy their own dependency needs and deflect the hostility of the leader. Separation from the person who started this process is viewed as much more of a direct, tangible loss than the loss of reality.

Identifying with the aggressor usually implies participating in his or her persecutory fantasies. The shared delusions are usually kept well within the realms of possibility and are based on actual past events or certain common expectations. Because the accusations contain an element of reality, the existence of this process may be difficult to discern. Through participation in such fantasies, subordinates maintain their source of gratification, lower their anxiety and guilt level, and express their anger in a deflected form by directing it toward others. The process is mirrorlike: the actions of the initiator of the process become reflected in those of the subordinates and vice versa and can be viewed as the outcome of an effort to save the alliance from breaking up.

Getting Trapped

In organizations, folie à deux contributes to the F-dimension. Often, however, this dimension of leadership is not seen for what it is, and contagious behavior patterns are more often than not accepted and rationalized as mere side products of an eccentric or autocratic leadership style.

To come back to our example of the first Henry Ford, one can view the relationship between him and his lieutenants Liebold, Sorensen, and, particularly, Bennett in the context of folie à deux. While at one point there may have been an element of reality in some of Ford's notions (for example, his concern about the power of the labor union movement), over time what reality there was got lost. Executives who did not participate in the idiosyncracies of Henry Ford and his close associates were fired. We have mentioned earlier how the Model T, which carried the company to its original success, eventually became a burden. Regardless, reinforced in his behavior by his close subordinates, Henry Ford, demonstrating a paranoid control-oriented disposition, stuck to his original strategy of a cheap car for the masses, making even suggestions of slight modifications taboo. Only in 1927, after the Model T had been in production for nineteen years, and only after an incredible loss of market share to General Motors—a development he had denied—was Henry Ford willing to make a model change.

This example illustrates how contagious a senior executive's behavior can be and how originally functional behavior can become increasingly damaging to the organization and even bring the company close to bankruptcy. Henry Ford's subordinates encouraged his views, although it remains open to question which subordinates were only conforming and which truly believed in what they were doing.

A more contemporary example involves the behavior of a senior executive of an isolated plant in a mining community in northern Canada who developed the belief that the head office wanted to close down the production facility. The introduction by the head office of a new factory control system triggered this idea, and regular visits by head office staff to implement the new control system only reinforced his belief, which he communicated to his subordinates and which was widely accepted. Although the production figures were more than adequate, collusion began to develop among plant personnel to protect their jobs. Eventually, the plant manager and his subordinates began to falsify information to show the plant in an even more favorable light. Only a spot check by the internal auditor of the head office brought these malpractices to light.

In many instances of folie à deux, a major question remains. How much of the behavior of subordinates can be accurately described in the context of folie à deux, and how much is mere compliance with an eccentric leadership style of a leader? The latter situation is illustrated by this example: The division head of a company in the machine tool industry would habitually mention the advanced technology used in his plants to each visitor to the company and at talks at trade association meetings. On promotion trips abroad, he was always trying to obtain license arrangements for his technology. And occasionally he would be successful. But, in spite of the fact that the company was turning out a high-quality product, there was nothing unique about the technology. As a matter of fact, most competitors were using comparable or even more advanced technological processes. Although most of his subordinates were aware of the actual state of affairs, they were unwilling to confront the division head with the facts. Compliance seemed easier than confrontation.

It is worth noting that mere compliance, if continued long enough, can evolve into stronger alliances, possibly resulting in active participation in these irrational actions; if co-opted long enough, one might eventually become a believer. These examples also emphasize some of the characteristics of folie à deux: for example, the relative isolation of the principal actors, their closeness, the existence of a dominant partner, and the emergence of delusionary ideas. The more recent Iran-Nicaragua arms deal scandal is only the latest, if one of the most grandiose, in a long series of such incidents where the right ambiance existed to make the unbelievable come true.

The Search for Scapegoats

Interactions that contain elements of folie à deux can contribute to collusion among subgroups to foster and maintain organizational myths and fantasies often only remotely related to the reality of the situation. In these instances, for some cliques, the organization's overall objectives and

127

strategies become of lesser interest than tactical considerations. The more concern for the maintenance of various irrational notions consumes their energy, the less congruence exists between specific actions and available information.

The members of these groups appear to live in a polarized world that no longer includes compromise or the acceptance of differences. Everyone is pressured to choose sides. It is also a world where one has to be continuously on one's guard against being singled out as a target for unfriendly actions. In such an organization, scapegoating becomes a predominant activity directed not only toward individuals within the organization but also toward such groups as the government, labor unions, competitors, suppliers, customers, or consumer organizations. What may have been a well-thought-out program may become distorted. For instance, alertness to the environment, which at one time may have been an organizational strength, can turn into a watch for imminent attack—a caricature of its original purpose.

Because of structural arrangements, subgroups frequently overlap with departments or other units. When this happens, people jealously guard areas of responsibility; territorialism prevails. The determination of boundaries among departments can lead to disputes. Seeking or accepting help from other groups may be considered a weakness or even a betrayal.

For example, in a large electronics company a senior vice-president of production development began to imagine that two of her colleagues, a vice-president of R&D and a vice-president of manufacturing, wanted to get rid of her. She perceived that her two colleagues were trying to reorganize her department out of existence and incorporate it into their own functional areas. At every available opportunity, she communicated this concern to her subordinates and expected them to confirm her suspicions. Disagreement was not tolerated; resistance resulted in either dismissal or transfer to another department. Gradually, many of her executives began to believe in her statements and to develop a siege mentality that led to a strong sense of group cohesion.

Relationships between this group and members of other departments became strained. What were once minor interdepartmental skirmishes deteriorated into open warfare. Committee meetings with members of other departments became public accusation sessions about the withholding of information, inaccurate data, and intrusion into each other's territory. In addition, because of her recurring complaints about poor quality of delivered material and late deliveries, the senior vice-president's contacts with some of her suppliers deteriorated. (A subsequent examination by a new vice-president found that most of these accusations were unwarranted.)

Eventually, managers of other departments began to avoid contact with product development people, thereby confirming their suspicions. Over time, the rest of the company built up a number of separate, fairly informal information systems to avoid any dealings with the product development group. Finally, after the product development group had made a number of budgetary mistakes because of distorted information, the president transferred the senior vice-president and reorganized the department.

In this example we can see how excessive rivalry and suspicion can lead people to adopt a narrow perspective of organizational priorities and become defensive and

129

controlling. Without integrating mechanisms to counter-balance their effect, these attitudes can cause dangerous divisions in an organization. Understandably, organizational participants will take refuge in politics and procedures, collusive activities, and other forms of organizational gamesmanship. Cooperation will disappear and priorities will become distorted.

Where elements of folie à deux seep into organizations, it can be seen as a failure of leadership. Conflict becomes stifling, creativity is discouraged, and distrust becomes the prevailing attitude. Instead of taking realistic action, executives react to emergencies by withdrawing or scapegoating. Fear is the undercurrent of the overall organizational climate. As ends and means become indistinguishable, the organization drifts along, losing touch with originally defined corporate goals and strategies.

MANAGEMENT OF FOLIE À DEUX

If a folie à deux pattern can be seen to exist in an organization, what can be done to cope with it? How can executives prevent themselves from getting stuck in this peculiar circular process? How can they recognize the symptoms?

Before outlining the steps executives can take, I want to stress that some aspects of what might look like folie à deux are not always organizationally undesirable. In the initial phases, interpersonal processes that could lead to folie à deux may be a source of strength, contributing to team building, commitment to goals and strategies, or even the establishment of effective environmental scanning mechanisms. Unfortunately, in the long run, interpersonal

130

relationships that in extreme form typify folie à deux may become a danger to the organization's operations and even its survival.

Executives likely to initiate this type of behavior usually show personality characteristics of a particularly narcissistic and paranoid nature. For example, they may appear to possess a lot of personal charm and seductiveness, qualities that may have originally been responsible for their rise in the organization. A closer look, however, will reveal that this behavior is often a cover-up for attitudes of conceit, arrogance, demonstrative self-sufficiency, and self-righteousness. Hyperalertness, hypersensitivity, and suspicion of others are other common characteristics. Moreover, individuals prone to folie à deux find it extremely difficult to alter their concepts and ideas; their actions often contain a rigid quality.

Since the paranoid style is the more manifest pattern among the instigators of folie à deux, when this process starts to spread, those influenced by it may show a similar pattern but in most instances not of such an intensive nature as the instigator. For all the participants in this form of mental contagion, however, a key problem remains the existence of highly ungratified dependency needs. It is exactly those needs that the instigators of this process fulfill. By being assertive, self-assured, and willing to take complete control, these executives attract those followers who need to be treated this way.

The danger signals of folie à deux can also be detected by looking at possible peculiarities of the organization's culture and ways of operation. One symptom is unusual selection and promotion procedures that largely reflect leaders' idiosyncracies rather than a concern for a candidate's overall managerial capabilities. Strange, selective, and unsystematic decision-making patterns, erratic information systems, excessive control, and extreme secrecy can also often be taken as danger signs.

Other indications may be a department's preoccupation with details at the cost of overall company effectiveness, and excessive manifestation of various stress symptoms in the organization, such as a large turnover of executives and a high degree of absenteeism, or labor turmoil. One can also view frequent changes in organizational goals, and the existence of grandiose, unrealistic plans, elaborate information systems (which often ignore essential strategic issues), and insistence on supposed conspiracies or the actual creation of such, as other signs.

Whatever the exact nature of the disturbing behavior pattern or process one notices, one should keep folie à deux processes in mind as a possible cause. Once symptoms are recognized, executives need to take corrective action, as well as to design systems and procedures that will counteract folie à deux.

In one instance, the president of a small biogenetics company became more and more distressed at the increasing financial strain on the company, developing a not completely unrealistic fear of being removed. A scientist himself, he had been the first to see the commercial value of a number of successfully completed genetic experiments and had gathered a group of like-minded individuals around him to commercialize the idea. His input in setting up the company and making it take off had been invaluable. Recently, however, he had become increasingly anxious. Investors had been pumping money into the company for a considerable length of time and he felt that their patience

132

was coming to an end. Although the company's products showed great promise in the laboratory, they had not yet been able to make a commercial breakthrough. More work in production technology was needed before the products would be ready for mass production.

The desire to perform and get into the black proved to be too much for the president of this company. In his wish for success he sincerely began to believe that they had finally turned the corner, that they had overcome the production difficulties. Although initially skeptical, eventually most people in the company began to share his optimism. Nonetheless, a few employees cautioned that they were still far away from a production breakthrough. But this he refused to believe and he exerted great pressure on these individuals to agree with his point of view.

The few disagreeing executives managed, however, to bring the matter to the attention of one of the key investors. When he realized what was happening, he put enough pressure on the president—while reassuring him, telling him how much he appreciated his efforts—to have him take on a consultant to advise him on production technology.

The consultant was quite aware of the situation and went ahead very carefully. Through her questioning she forced the executives in the company to really think through their assumptions. Doing so helped them refocus on realistic time and production schedules. Just as important, the chance to share his worries with the consultant took a lot of pressure from the president. It also made him aware that the investors recognized his talent and his efforts, and really wanted him to succeed. Furthermore, he began to realize that they were not as impatient as he had imagined. This awareness calmed him down and led to a new element of realism in the company. It was as if a magical spell had been broken. Although the situation remained difficult for some time, with the help of the consultant and the support of the investors, the company finally made a commercial breakthrough and became profitable.

We can see how in this case enough outside leverage existed and the CEO had enough contact with reality to be brought back. Both factors conspired to make change feasible. However, when folie à deux is in full swing the leader involved may be beyond helping himself. For the person who started this process, the route back to reality can be very difficult: a disposition toward delusional thinking is not easy to overcome. Appeal to the leader's logic and reality does not help; on the contrary, it might evoke uncompromising, hostile, and aggressive reactions. Rather, in these instances, one should, if possible, first establish some degree of trust and closeness with affected leaders as in the example, avoiding emotive subjects but discussing small unimportant changes. This will help make them willing to entertain the possibility that their assumptions of the organizational environment are invalid, and eventually may help them accept large important changes.

This change in attitudes is not going to be arrived at easily, but without it, it will not be possible for an affected manager to make a realistic self-appraisal of inner strengths and weaknesses. Substituting reality for fantasies is likely to be a slow and difficult process involving the reintegration and adjustment of many deeply ingrained behavior patterns. Because of the intensity of the delusions, in many instances these persons may need professional guidance.

The outlook for the affected followers is more positive and usually less dramatic. Their disposition is more of the dependent type. Frequently, merely the removal of the closeness with the affected senior executive will be sufficient to break the magic spell. Some form of disorientation may occur at the beginning, but proper guidance by other unaffected executives will soon help to bring the managers back into more normal, reality-orientated behavior patterns.

Obviously, coping with folie à deux in an organization is particularly difficult when the instigator is a powerful senior executive who is also a major shareholder. Occasionally, however, in such instances the support of a countervailing power such as the government or a union makes it possible to guide the organization away from possible self-destructive adventures. Other interested parties who could blow the whistle are customers, suppliers, and bankers.

The situation becomes somewhat less problematic when the chief executive officer is not a major shareholder, since the board of directors and the shareholders can play a more active monitoring role. One of their responsibilities is to watch for possible danger signs. Naturally, the possibility always exists that board members will be drawn into the delusionary activities of a senior executive, but this is less likely to happen with a board of outside directors with diverse backgrounds. Such a board may be able to neutralize a folie à deux process.

Organizational solutions to folie à deux become more feasible when the instigator is not a senior executive officer. Then confrontation, transfer, or, in serious cases, dismissal is sufficient to stop the process. Also important, however, are the systems and procedures in an organization. The organizational culture and structure can be reoriented. Objective information systems can also assist managers to focus on reality, as can using many different sources for information gathering and processing. Interdepartmental committees and formal control systems can fulfill a similar function. Pressures toward more participative management are other ways of preventing, or at least limiting, the emergence or proliferation of folie à deux. These structural changes can reduce the power of leaders and restrict the advantage they may take of their subordinates' dependency needs.

Supporting individual responsibility and independence of mind in the organization, as well as selecting and promoting managers who behave accordingly, can be a buffer against folie à deux. An organizational culture of mutual collaboration, delegation, open conflict resolution, and respect for individuality will expose a process of mental contagion before it can spread. Such organizational patterns lessen dependency needs and force conflict into the open, thus counteracting the incidence of vicious circles in interpersonal behavior.

One type of organization that seems more susceptible to folie à deux than others—showing the F-dimension in full bloom—is the entrepreneurial one. This type of organization tends to have a high concentration of power, and given the often domineering personality of the entrepreneur may attract individuals with highly frustrated dependency needs. The kind of organizational culture created by entrepreneurs therefore warrants special attention.

7
The Dark Side of Entrepreneurship

Willy was a salesman. And for a salesman, there is no rock bottom to life. He don't put a bolt to a nut, he don't tell you the law or give you medicine. He's a man way out there in the blue, riding on a smile and a shoeshine.

Arthur Miller, *The Death of a Salesman*

K aren Star had come to the Salar Corporation as vice-president of operations after a period of intense lobbying by its president, Lester Milton. An entrepreneur with ambitious ventures in mind for the future of his company, Lester had painted a bright picture of its prospects and the opportunities Karen would find to exercise her managerial skills. The sky seemed the limit as Lester projected things. And when Karen had first come to work, her arrival had created a lot of excitement and anticipation. She had worked hard, put in long hours, and for over three months had been in almost daily contact with her boss. But suddenly, all that had changed. After having been treated like the long-awaited heroine, Karen suddenly realized that the honeymoon was over—she was left in the cold. Lester hardly had time to see her. She had to admit she felt let down, and wondered if she should have taken this job in the first place.

Her first assignment had been to set up a new budgeting system. It was an idea she had come up with after looking at the old system and seeing how outdated it was, given Salar's current operations. When Karen had pointed out to

Lester how little information the old system was giving them and had outlined her plan for revising it, Lester had been so enthusiastic in his response that he had wanted it done yesterday. Karen had come to the realization that Lester was not a patient man. You never had to wait long for his answers; he was a person who operated on hunches and impressions. He liked dramatic, instant action.

With hindsight Karen realized that the system she had installed might be too sophisticated for Salar, but nevertheless, it was a good system. Of course, the message she was getting now from the president was quite different. After installing the system, Karen had discovered, paradoxically enough, that the Salar Corporation was actually losing money. Her boss did not take this piece of information lightly. He turned on Karen as a bringer of bad news. To her great surprise, Karen discovered that of all people responsible, she was being blamed for the company's losses. In short, she was told that things were out of control because her systems change had "thrown things into confusion."

Karen knew that the changeover had little to do with it. A previous vice-president had made some serious merchandising errors: his key mistakes had been faulty pricing decisions and large raw material purchases that turned out to be wasteful. Judging by the stories going around the office, he had certainly fooled Lester with his forecasts of how profitable the various product lines were going to be. He seemed to have been one of the few able to wind the president around his little finger. In any event, the results of all Karen's efforts were that her responsibilities were curtailed and she was excluded from a sizable part of top management decision making. Planning was taken abruptly out of her jurisdiction and given back to a colleague who was an old-timer. To add insult to injury, she was the last person to be informed.

During the five months she had been with Salar, a number of things she observed had troubled Karen. The organizational culture was in sharp contrast to that of the publicly owned corporation where she had worked before. The differences all seemed to center around trust. She was beginning to wonder if Lester Milton really had much faith in anyone. One symptom of his lack of confidence in his people was his insistence on being kept informed of the minutest details of the operations. Karen would get annoyed at being asked repeatedly, as other subordinates were also, to come to Lester's office to explain trivial decisions. It was disrupting to the flow of work in the office. And you had little choice: if you didn't keep Lester informed and something went wrong, all hell would break loose. If it was bad news, the unexpected was definitely not welcomed. Subordinates would often paint too rosy a picture after agonizing over how to present unpleasant information to Lester, which inevitably led to distortions and the creation of false optimism. Karen felt that although Lester's controlling style may have been useful when his company was smaller, it was now getting seriously in the way of sound decision making. As she looked around, Karen questioned how much tolerance her boss really had for independent thinking. Colleagues who were old-timers seemed extremely subservient, too eager to please Lester. If they had opinions of their own, they were unwilling to stand up for them.

At first Karen had not paid much attention to Lester's descriptions of himself as a workaholic. She had been caught up in the excitement of working with him, and in

141

the possibilities she saw for Salar's growth and expansion as well as for her own career. Now she wondered how Lester could have any family life, considering the long hours he spent at the office and the time out on business trips. And he expected his key executives to be similarly dedicated and available at all times. If Karen ever refused to be available, it was interpreted as insubordination. She soon learned it could produce outbursts of anger. Lester's leadership style—erratic, impulsive, and extreme—made Karen wonder if the job was worth the strain. She might as well start looking for another job.

Karen Star's dilemma is not unusual. Some entrepreneurs can create an organizational culture that makes adaptation very difficult. One should not, however, see such behavior as the norm. Many entrepreneurs are well equipped to deal with different company environments.

But nevertheless, the question remains: What are entrepreneurs like? What distinguishes them from other business people? Although as a group they are not easy to get a handle on, some characteristics seem to be common to all of them. For example, entrepreneurs seem to be achievement-oriented, like to take responsibility for decisions, and dislike repetitive, routine work. Creative entrepreneurs possess high levels of energy and great degrees of perseverance and imagination, which, combined with a willingness to take moderate, calculated risks enable them to transform what often begins as a very simple, ill-defined idea into something concrete. Entrepreneurs can also instill highly contagious enthusiasm in an organization. They convey a sense of purpose and by doing so, convince others that they are where the action is. Entrepreneurs have the seductiveness, gamesmanship, or charisma it takes to lead an organization and give it momentum.

Along with their mystique, however, entrepreneurs can have personality quirks that make them hard people to work for or with. For example, their bias toward action may make them act rather thoughtlessly, and this can have dire consequences for the organization. Moreover, some entrepreneurs have great difficulty taking advice. As F. Derek du Toit, an entrepreneur himself, admits, "the entrepreneur who starts his own business generally does so because he is a difficult employee. He does not take kindly to suggestions or orders from other people and aspires most of all to run his own shop.... His idiosyncrasies do not hurt anybody so long as the business is small, but once the business gets larger, requiring the support and active cooperation of more people, he is at risk if he does not change his approach. It has been correctly stated that the biggest burden a growing company faces is having a full-blooded entrepreneur as its owner.

Du Toit raises the question of what you should look out for if you are considering working for an entrepreneur, taking one on board, or encouraging new ventures. What can cause problems? Are there pitfalls to avoid? If so, what are the options in such situations? What provisions can you make to accommodate the typical entrepreneur? Do entrepreneurs have more personal problems than other people? In short, what is the dark side of entrepreneurship? Why are entrepreneurs particularly susceptible to the F-dimension?

CHAPTER 7

THE ENTREPRENEUR'S THEATER

In answering these questions, let's keep in mind that entrepreneurs are not a homogeneous group. They come in all shapes and sizes, each with his or her own characteristics.

Ambivalence about Control

A significant theme in the life and personality of many entrepreneurs is ambivalence about control. At times, their preoccupation with control affects their ability to take direction or give it appropriately and has serious implications for how they get along with others. Some entrepreneurs are seemingly torn when an issue of control surfaces: they are filled with fantasies of grandiosity, influence, power, and authority, yet also feel helpless. They seem to fear that their grandiose desires will get out of control and place them ultimately at the mercy of others.

Consequently, some entrepreneurs have serious difficulty addressing issues of dominance and submission and are suspicious of authority. This attitude contrasts greatly with that of managers. While managers seem able to identify in a positive and constructive way with authority figures, using them as role models, many entrepreneurs lack managers' fluidity in changing from a superior to a subordinate role. Instead, they often experience structure as stifling. They find it very difficult to work with others in structured situations unless they are the ones who created the structure in the first place and work is done on their terms.

Larry Malcolm, a successful entrepreneur in the sporting goods industry, is a typical example. Larry had always found it difficult to work for others. After he dropped out of college, Malcolm started work as a sporting goods salesperson for a department store. He liked the experience (sports had always been his great enthusiasm), but a fight with the department head over the right way of displaying merchandise prematurely ended his stay. He then found a clerical position in an apparel company that manufactured active wear. Although he managed to stay on longer at this job, he disliked the working environment, felt stifled, and finally quit.

In his third job, he didn't fare much better. But by this time, Malcolm began to realize that working for others was not his forte. Not knowing what to do and wanting time to think about the future, he took his savings and made an extensive trip to Europe. At a sporting goods fair in Germany, he met a designer whose work he liked, and on the basis of the man's designs, managed to get a few orders from a department store and a number of small retail operations when he returned to the States. All of a sudden, Malcolm found himself running his own business.

Larry Malcom's story is not unusual. Many entrepreneurs seem to be driven by a magnificent obsession, or dream: some idea, concept, or theme that haunts them and that eventually determines what kind of business they choose to be in. Malcolm's great passion was sports and everything related to it. This obsession partially explains his talent for finding more functional as well as attractive designs. This focused interest is not the only factor, however. Listening to entrepreneurs' case histories, I have found many situations where it was also, as for Malcolm, the individual's inability to submit to authority and accept organizational rules that drove him or her to become an entrepreneur.

Many entrepreneurs seem to be misfits who need to create their own environment. Offering the deference a subordinate usually owes a superior often suffocates this type of person. They tell themselves that they don't want to be at the mercy of others. Even if they move away from old controlling influences, these concerns linger on. Many entrepreneurs are preoccupied with the threat of subjection to some external control or infringement on their will. When such people are suddenly placed in a subordinate position, power conflicts are inevitable.

People who are overly concerned about being in control also have little tolerance for subordinates who think for themselves. In organizations, this desire for control can lead to extreme behavior: for instance, an owner-manager needing to be informed about even the most minute operation of the company.

To illustrate: Every morning one entrepreneur responsible for a twenty-million-dollar consumer product operation habitually opened not only his own personal mail but all mail directed to the company. In addition, he insisted on approving all requisitions, no matter how small. He said it gave him a feel for the overall functioning of the organization.

Once that may have been the case. But the excessive concern with detail that may be appropriate in the start-up phase of a company increasingly becomes a burden to the organization as it stifles the information flow, hampers decision making, and inhibits the attraction and retention of capable managers. In this entrepreneur's situation, although his subordinates admired many of his qualities, they deeply resented being treated as children. Good performers did not stay.

Moreover, because true accountability was lacking, information needed for decision making did not circulate. As a result, sales and profits plateaued and the future growth of the enterprise was endangered. Buyers of entrepreneurial companies started by such people should be prepared to inherit a mediocre management group.

Sense of Distrust

Closely related to the need for control is a proclivity toward suspicion of others. Some entrepreneurs stand out as extreme examples due to their strong distrust of the world around them. They live in fear of being victimized. They want to be ready should disaster strike. Paradoxically, some seem to feel best when their fortunes are at their lowest. Like many other leaders, when at the top of the success wave they imagine themselves incurring the envy of others, and become anxious.

So as not to tempt the wrath of the gods, when people ask them how things are, they respond by saying that business is only "so-so" or "not too bad." But if their fortunes turn and they are close to bankruptcy, they feel as if they have paid the price, done their penance for having been successful. Because it produces a sense of relief, their predicament can have a positive effect. With the alleviation of anxiety, they have the energy to start anew, which they do with enthusiasm and a sense of purpose.

People who act this way are continually scanning the environment for something to confirm their suspicions. This behavior pattern does, of course, have its constructive side: it makes the entrepreneur alert to the moves of competitors, suppliers, customers, or government that affect the industry. Anticipating the actions of others protects them from being taken unaware. But such vigilance can also lead them to lose any sense of proportion. Focusing on certain trouble spots and ignoring others, entrepreneurs like this may blow up trivial things and lose sight of the reality of the situation.

When a strong sense of distrust assisted by a need for control takes over, the consequences for the organization are serious: sycophants set the tone, people stop acting independently, and political gamesmanship is rampant. Such entrepreneurs can interpret harmless acts as threats to their control and see them as warranting destructive counteractions. Understandably, such thinking doesn't lead to sound head office–subsidiary relationships in situations where an entrepreneurial firm has been taken over and the entrepreneur has been asked to stay on.

In one case, headquarters sent a consultant to help the chief executive of a newly acquired company to assess profitability by product line and develop and implement a strategic plan. When the consultant arrived, the ex-owner didn't even let him look at the financial statements, on the grounds (as he explained to headquarters) that the consultant might use the information to help the competition. At another time, when his machines were idle and he had to lay off employees, this same person refused to sell goods-in-process to a noncompeting business. He argued that he once had been burned when a competitor used his goods-in-process to manufacture a line of products that competed with his own, and he was not going to let it happen again.

In another case, one of the principals of a consulting firm was surprised to discover that their client had television cameras monitoring the front and back entries of both his plant and his office building. To allay his fears that employees were stealing from him, the entrepreneur kept two split-screen consoles on his desk and watched them constantly.

The problem one has countering such distorted forms of reasoning and action is that behind the fear and suspicion always lies some reality. If one looks hard enough, one will always find somewhere some confirmation of the entrepreneur's suspicions—someone stealing something. Unfortunately, the person who manages in this way forgets the price the company pays in deteriorating morale, low employee satisfaction, and declining production.

Desire for Applause

The common heroic myth begins with the hero's humble birth, rapid rise to prominence and power, conquest of the forces of evil, vulnerability to the sin of pride, and, finally, fall through betrayal or heroic sacrifice. The basic symbolic themes here—of birth, conquest, pride, betrayal, and death —are relevant to all of us. And as we have seen, some entrepreneurs act out the same myth, with a Greek chorus in the background applauding their achievements but warning them about pride.

The myth helps us to see why quite a few entrepreneurs live with a great amount of tension. They feel they're living on the edge, that their success will not last (their need

149

for control and their sense of distrust are symptomatic of this anxiety); but they also have an overriding narcissistic concern to be heard and recognized, to be seen as heroes. Some entrepreneurs need to show others that they amount to something, that they cannot be ignored.

A very gifted entrepreneur who was experiencing great stress while working out how fast to expand his business, described to me a dream he had had repeatedly. In the dream, he would be standing on a balcony, looking down to see a group of women smiling admiringly up at him. This scene would soon fade and the admirers would turn into harpies. Feeling suffocated, he would wake up screaming. He also recalled dreams of himself as a swaggering cowboy climbing an ever-narrowing trail leading to the top of a mountain. But below the top, a gate blocked the road. To move past it, the man would have to risk sliding down.

If one looks at these dreams as symbolic, albeit in a simplified way, one sees some wishes and fears standing out. One of the more noticeable characteristics of both dreams is their grandiosity: they both involve high positions —balcony and mountains—the way to which is fraught with many dangers. We want to ask, Why does he want to go there at all? Whom is he trying to impress? What are the dangers? How do women figure in all of it? What is the role of men? What makes him scream, and what causes the feelings of suffocation? What rationale lies behind his hyperactivity?

Perhaps one way of looking at the need for applause is to see it as a narcissistic reaction against feeling insignificant, like a nothing. Some entrepreneurs hear an inner voice that tells them they will never amount to anything. But regardless of who put this idea into their minds, these people are not retiring types who take such a rebuke passively; they are the defiant, reactive ones who deal with it creatively through action. They possess enough inner strength to prove the voice wrong and show the world that they do amount to something. They will ride to the top in spite of all dangers; they will get the applause; they will find a way to master their fears.

A manifestation of this need is the interest some entrepreneurs show in building monuments as symbols of their achievements. Sometimes the monument is an imposing office building or production facility; sometimes it is a product that takes on symbolic significance. For example, because he wanted to show people in the section of town where he grew up that he had amounted to something, one entrepreneur built an imposing head office and new factory. The contrast between his building and the decrepit surroundings was striking. That this action jeopardized the company's financial position—it was during a period of economic decline and all advisers advocated offshore production—made the decision even more bizarre.

Given these strong needs, it's reasonable to ask if it is possible to harness such drives. Can entrepreneurs relinquish their need to invest in certain organizational symbols? Can they live under the constraints of corporate budgets, expense controls, and long-range plans? Can they modify their narcissistic needs? Can they play second fiddle?

Defensive Processes

Splitting—the tendency to see things in extremes when dealing with other people—is a common defensive pattern

151

among entrepreneurs. They idealize some people and put them on a pedestal, and vilify others. The attitudinal pendulum shifts all too easily. Let's look at an example. One entrepreneur made a point of hiring young MBAs just out of school. He would marvel at their mastery of the latest management techniques and hold the new executives up as examples for his other employees. He would tell them that these were the kinds of managers he needed. Inevitably, his lavish praise would stir up enormous resentment among the rest of the staff (with the predictable spiteful consequences). But also, just as inevitably, the president's infatuation with his latest recruit would soon exhaust itself and disappointment would set in. No new recruit could live up to the president's exaggerated expectations, and eventually, like the other MBAs before, he or she would leave.

When this same man sold his company, he was at first quite enamored of the acquiring company's CEO. He would praise his new boss's accomplishments to all. It would give him great pleasure to dwell on certain incidents illustrating the CEO's achievements. But as with all the others, this infatuation did not last long. A request from headquarters for more information about a new advertising campaign was the turning point. The ex-owner interpreted the request as a vote of no confidence, as an attempt to find fault with his actions, and even as part of a plan to get rid of him. He reacted similarly to other requests from headquarters. Almost overnight in his eyes, the CEO changed from hero to chief villain. Eventually, because the entrepreneur withheld information, the CEO had no choice but to make his fears come true, and he let the entrepreneur go.

As described earlier, we all have a tendency to externalize internal problems: we project our discomforts and fears onto others. When we attribute a felt threat to someone else or to an event, it becomes more manageable. But if this tendency toward projection becomes exaggerated and the predominant reaction to stressful circumstances, it can be problematic. Scapegoating is a method people commonly adopt to see themselves as blameless and feel virtuous. If used to the extreme, though, this way of managing stress becomes a dysfunctional personality characteristic.

People who act in this way experience little sense of personal responsibility. They distance themselves from the problem and deny and rationalize away whatever responsibility they may have had. They refuse to see what they don't like to see and blame others. In an organization, this kind of thinking contributes to political infighting, to denial of responsibility, and to insularity and factionalism.

Finally, quite a few entrepreneurs are inclined to turn the passive into the active, a characteristic that relates to their difficulty with controlling their impulses and managing anxiety and depression. Such entrepreneurs defend against anxiety (evidenced by their restlessness and irritability) by turning to action—the manic defense—as an antidote.

As these entrepreneurs try to steer between their fear of success and fear of failure, and wonder if success will last or whether they will suffer from the dreaded fate of the mythical hero, they finally can't stand the tension. They flee into action, even if it is impulsive and thoughtless, without considering facts. This is not to say that waiting out events has no attraction for them, only that they may fear so strongly that being passive would make them overdependent and, ultimately, controlled by others, that they have to act counterdependently.

Most of us work continually to keep a balance between dependency needs and the wish to do things on our own, to be independent. Some entrepreneurs seem to have a particularly rough time maintaining this balance and preserving a stable image of themselves. Instead, they seesaw and are prone to deep mood swings. When things are going well, everything is terrific. But when the bubble bursts and something goes wrong, the pendulum often shifts completely in the other direction. Then everything is terrible, the situation is hopeless, and bankruptcy is just around the corner.

One entrepreneur fought depressive feelings by resorting to manic, hyperactive behavior. Given his difficulties in tolerating bad news, he would continuously reassure himself that everything was going fine. He would describe at great length how fantastically successful and profitable his company was. In this state of mind, letting himself see only what he wanted to see and using all the defensive patterns I have just described, he didn't bother to read sales and financial reports. If anyone questioned him about this he would say that his reporting system was just fine; everything was terrific. Only news from his accountants pointing out that the company had suffered a loss during the last quarter aroused him, finally, from his self-deceptive state. Needless to say, he didn't take the report with equanimity; his mood plunged. He feared that he was out of his depth and that his operation was finished. It took him some time to pull himself together.

ENTREPRENEURIAL FOLIE À DEUX

I indicated earlier that because of the great intensity and closeness that develop in small isolated groups, entrepreneurial ventures tend to be particularly susceptible to folie à deux behavior patterns. Let's take an example: The president and founder of a medium-sized electronics company often expressed concern about the need for more professional management in her company. She liked to state that the entrepreneurial phase had passed and that the time had come to make organizational changes, prepare to go public, and plan for succession. To that end, she engaged in a strong recruitment effort. Her charismatic appeal and strong advocacy of professional management attracted a great number of new executives. Their influx was balanced, however, by a steady exodus of many of the same executives who soon realized how difficult it was to conform to the president's demands.

Calling the company "a happy family," the founder felt she could intrude into the private family affairs of her subordinates. While she promised that she would delegate a great deal of responsibility to newcomers, this turned out to be poorly defined assignments without much authority, which frequently led to failure. A person's career advancement depended on his or her closeness to the president, compliance with her wishes, and willingness to participate in often irrational behavior patterns. Exile to various obscure sales offices became the price of resistance. Eventually, the company had to pay a toll for this leadership, but the president blamed the steady drop in sales and profits on government intervention, union activities, and sabotage by a number of singled-out employees.

Hoarding information, playing favorites, inconsistent handling of company policies, and, generally, creating ambiguous situations do seem to be common problems for leaders in entrepreneurial companies. Because the com-

155

pany's survival depends on the entrepreneur, many subordinates are easily drawn into supporting him or her even when his or her behavior is irrational. Those unwilling to participate leave, while conformers and ones susceptible to folie à deux relationships remain.

This phenomenon may explain why in so many entrepreneurial companies a strong layer of capable middle managers is missing. In situations of folie à deux, those who remain spend a great part of their energies on political infighting and supporting the irrational behavior and beliefs of the entrepreneur. These activities can become even more intense if members of the entrepreneur's family are employed in the company so that family and organizational dynamics become closely intertwined.

TURNING ON THE LIGHT

I have described how the entrepreneur can fall victim to the F-dimension. The cases I've outlined here are extreme. For one thing, many countervailing forces—institutions, government, banks, and a person's health and good judgment—prevent excesses. Most entrepreneurs' sense of reality prevents things from getting out of hand.

Entrepreneurs do not necessarily have more personal problems than other people, nor do they inevitably have personality disorders. One can extract from the previous discussion, however, that entrepreneurs have their own unique ways of dealing with the stresses and strains of daily life. In saying this, I want to reemphasize that the boundaries between very creative and aberrant behavior can be blurry; normal and irrational behavior are not discrete categories on a scale. The mix of the creative and the irrational is what makes entrepreneurs tick and accounts for their many positive contributions. Entrepreneurs create new industries and jobs and stimulate the economy. Their visionary qualities and leadership abilities enable those around them to transcend petty concerns and attain great achievements.

In one case the president of a conglomerate worked hard to build a relationship based on mutual trust with the entrepreneur running a company he was considering acquiring. The two talked about the working arrangements and operational procedures each would accept. While the entrepreneur expressed his concern about preserving his independence, the president described the information he would need from any subsidiary to make him feel comfortable. They also agreed that the entrepreneur could call on the president any time for assistance.

After the acquisition, the president kept his promise to let the entrepreneur run his own show; he kept interference from headquarters at a minimum. The arrangement about assistance turned out to be critical. The entrepreneur used the president regularly as a sounding board, which he did not mind since it enabled him, in an atmosphere of mutual trust, to bring a healthy dose of reality to the entrepreneur's occasionally high-flying schemes. This loose-tight arrangement turned out to be very successful. The new acquisition became one of the most profitable in the conglomerate's portfolio of companies.

Unfortunately, stories about entrepreneurs don't always have happy endings. The personality quirks I have described can make collaboration very trying. The last case provides a clue, however, as to how executives and venture

157

capitalists can work with these imaginative, but sometimes difficult, people. The challenge is to develop a relationship based on mutual trust that allows the executive and the entrepreneur to talk openly and regularly and that enables the latter to test ideas against reality.

To facilitate this process, venture capitalists and chief executives should respect the entrepreneur's needs for independence and design control and information systems accordingly. Living with such an arrangement is not easy. Given the erratic way some entrepreneurs run their companies, a loosely coupled relationship with headquarters may be too much to handle for many executives. Such an approach demands that executives at the head office maintain a proper balance between monitoring performance and letting go of control. One way to ensure the autonomy of acquired companies is to keep the headquarters staff lean to prevent excessive interference.

Top managers should heed a few other precautions before taking an entrepreneur on board. Before buying an entrepreneurial company, they should pay close attention to the quality of management that will come with the deal. It is important to find out if the personnel pool of the company to be acquired can be trained and developed. Or is one faced with such mediocre management that it will be very difficult to build a team that will fit the acquiring company's culture? Does a situation of trained incapacity and "decidophobia" exist that will make it impossible for the acquired management group to move the company forward if the entrepreneur departs?

In case of acquisition, executives should also consider how well the entrepreneurial company's culture will fit the acquiring company's. Is the way of doing things at the head office very different at the acquired company? How similar are the basic values in the two organizations—for example, on issues like accepted behavior, structure, and goals? Corporate executives should be equally open to change; cultural adjustment works both ways. (I am not thinking here of a dramatic transformation but of a gradual shift.) In any case, executives need to consider whether the cultural differences are so great that a clash is inevitable. Moreover, if conflicts occur, will they be drawn out?

Any subordinate working for an entrepreneur should realize that he or she is in a vulnerable position. Very often he or she appears to be there at the pleasure of the entrepreneur. There may be times when the subordinate can bring about a change in the entrepreneur's attitude, but these changes tend to be modest. Whatever behavior modifications take place, the subordinate is up against the dynamics of power. Entrepreneurs control their companies in more than one way. More often than not, they are major shareholders, and subordinates have to take the consequences of their ownership position. The realization that they might lose control over their company if they continue to operate in an ineffective way, however, can motivate entrepreneurs to do something about their personal style and to take remedial action.

Individuals attracted to firms run by the kind of entrepreneurs I have described are often self-selected: many among them don't mind working under a strong leader. If they are searching for a symbolic parent figure, the entrepreneur is there to oblige. Instead of feeling held back or even misled by the peculiar behavior patterns of certain entrepreneurs, some individuals identify with them and draw strength from their leadership. This interface can con-

159

tribute to a constructive, synergistic relationship whereby the entrepreneur's vision and drive are translated into effective and efficient organizational functioning.

In most of the examples I have described, if anyone can influence the entrepreneur's leadership style, it is usually an outsider. Someone not heavily exposed to the organization's culture has the greatest impact. Such a person—a consultant, a banker, a member of an advisory board, or in the case of an acquisition, top executives of the acquiring company—often has enough distance to see things in perspective and to discount the drama and tension common in entrepreneurial firms. Such a person can play the role of confidant and use the entrepreneur's ambition to effect constructive change.

Given the wealth of product and market knowledge entrepreneurs usually have, separating them from their companies should not be the first option. Of course, in those instances where it becomes quickly obvious that an entrepreneur's need for autonomy overshadows everything else, it may be advisable to have the founder stay on for a short transition period only. Yet because, as a rule, acquiring companies do feel the need to impose their cultures on subsidiaries, entrepreneur-owners most often do leave. But when this all-too-familiar scenario takes place, usually new problems emerge, this time having to do with succession.

Whatever one finally decides to do, one should keep in mind that entrepreneurs' personality quirks may be responsible for their drive and energy and are important factors in making them so successful. Instead of fighting these idiosyncrasies, executives should regard developing them as a challenge.

A Chinese proverb says, "He who rides a tiger cannot dismount." That is what the entrepreneur is all about. The simultaneous desire for danger and opportunity is what makes for the entrepreneurial spirit, which in the end is the lifeblood of any society.

8
The Succession Game

"If the king begins to age his magical
strength is threatened; it may grow
weaker, or disappear, or evil powers
may turn it into its opposite. Therefore
the aging king's life must be taken and
his magical strength transferred to his
successor." The king's person is of
importance only as long as it is
undamaged: only as an intact vessel is it
capable of containing the forces of increase. The smallest defect renders the
king suspect to his subjects, for it means
he may lose some of the substance entrusted to him and so endanger the
welfare of his people. The constitution of
these kingdoms is the physical constitution of the king himself. He is sworn in
on condition, as it were, of his strength
and health. A king who shows grey
hairs, whose eyesight deteriorates, who

loses his teeth, or becomes impotent, is killed, or must commit suicide; he takes poison or is strangled. These are the usual forms of death, for the shedding of his blood is forbidden. Sometimes the length of his reign is fixed from the start: the kings of Jukun . . . originally ruled for seven years. Among the Bambara the newly elected king traditionally determined the length of his own reign. "A strip of cotton was put round his neck and two men pulled the ends in opposite directions whilst he himself took out of a calabash as many pebbles as he could grasp in his hand. These indicated the number of years he would reign, on the expiration of which he would be strangled."

Elias Canetti, *Crowds and Power*

S uch dramatic events do not happen in the business world, but this does not mean we cannot find parallels. Performance monitoring and ritual killings are not confined to ancient African kingdoms: the succession of a company president is not without drama of its own. We have seen how the succession of entrepreneurs in particular, given their emotional investment in their company, can lead to great drama. But leaders of publicly owned corporations are also no strangers to succession problems. Succession can be a period of great upheaval and conflict when emotions run high for successor, predecessor, and all others affected. Succession at the top can have a ripple effect throughout an entire organization bringing with it some profound strategic and structural changes.

Ed Nolan, one of the members of the board of Bohlton, a diversified paper products company, was wondering how to interpret the outcome of the latest board meeting. The main topic on the agenda had been the report of the executive selection committee presented by Bob Reed, chairman and CEO of Bohlton. Like most board members, Ed very much appreciated Bob's handling of the company. Bob

165

had certainly been its builder and prime mover and more than anyone else was responsible for its success. But since Bob was getting on in age, the question of what would happen after his departure had been increasingly troubling some of the board members. Had they been sufficiently vigilant about leadership succession? Had enough effort been made to develop executives with adequate stature and experience in the company to replace Bob? Or had the board been lulled to sleep by Bob's fine performance and good health?

Four years ago, with great trepidation, knowing Bob's attachment to the company, Ed had brought up the issue of retirement at a board meeting. He still vividly remembered Bob's reaction: it had been one of deep irritation. Bob had quickly brushed the matter aside with the comment that of course he had thought about it and had been looking into it. But that had seemed to be the end of the story; nothing else had happened. Eventually, getting frustrated, Ed and a few other board members had brought up the topic again, pointing out to Bob that he was fast approaching Bohlton's mandatory retirement age. Something had to be done. This time it looked as if they had had more effect. Their combined pressure had resulted in the formation of a selection committee headed by Bob. This had happened two years ago.

Ed could not but acknowledge that the selection committee had acted vigorously and seemed to have made a remarkable effort. From all the evidence at hand, the thoroughness of their search had known no bounds. Interviews and secret meetings had taken place. Consultants and headhunters had been used. One consultant had been retained and had even developed a sophisticated scoring grid, listing in an intricate way the required qualifications of potential candidates. Eventually, elaborate personality profiles had been made up about five candidates: three insiders and two outsiders. In spite of the secrecy, all these activities had not gone unnoticed in the company and had caused a lot of anticipation and tension among the senior executives.

The final results had been presented at the last board meeting. In spite of the intensive search effort, the board was told, not one of the candidates qualified. It was the selection committee's opinion that the three inside candidates needed at least four to six years more seasoning. The expertise of the outside candidates, in spite of outstanding track records, was not thought to be compatible with the future needs of the company. The board ended up agreeing that Bob put off his retirement for another four years.

In retrospect, Ed felt troubled by the decision. Something didn't feel quite right about it. Hadn't the time come for a change in leadership? Was it good for a company to have one person that long in charge? Were there really no competent candidates available? And why did no one qualify? What had happened to management development all these years? Furthermore, if there were no qualified inside candidates, there must have been competent outsiders. Did the person they were looking for really exist or was he or she a product of their combined imaginations? Had they been looking for a mythical figure combining the qualities of all the executives under consideration? Was it also possible that the members of the selection committee and the board were deliberately not dealing with the issue but instead colluding with the CEO, knowing Bob's attachment to his job and his reluctance to release the reins? Looking back, Ed wondered if the decision had really been in the best interests of the company. Could the board have acted earlier or differently?

Ed is not alone in his concerns. The described scenario is not that unusual. Some CEOs have a very hard time dealing with succession and retirement. Although they may give lip service to the matter, in many cases they avoid real action. As in this example, sometimes the key players (and that includes the board), willingly or not, may even collude with the CEO, going through drawn-out pseudoscientific selection methods that often turn out barren in the end. The result of this lack of action may be that when suddenly faced with a fait accompli due to death, illness, poor performance, or other dramatic causes, the succession decision has to be made at a very late stage, often under crisis conditions.

Succession is a very sensitive topic, and besides that, even when a real willingness to deal with the matter exists, its planning remains at best a very inexact science. And that is unfortunate, since poor succession planning has been called a major contributing factor to business failure. The way succession is handled has a great influence on the future viability of an enterprise. It has significant effects on the perceptions of investors and hence has serious financial performance implications.

A CEO's avoidance of or halfhearted efforts in dealing with succession planning is not the only problem; the decision whether to go for an insider or an outsider is another critical matter that can have serious repercussions within the corporation. A corollary to these problems is how the transition of leadership will be managed. What factors have to be taken into account during the transition? What are the critical issues?

Succession when it eventually takes place is usually a period of change. Traditional norms are disrupted. Strategic replacements occur that can affect the organization's structure and transform reporting relationships. Not only actual succession but even the rumor that succession is at hand can have dramatic consequences because of its anticipatory effects.

This is not to say that succession always has to be problematic. Many CEOs cope very successfully with the problem. In many companies, CEOs are bound by tradition or company policy to step down at a certain age, and plan accordingly. Many CEOs have enough vision and self-insight to transcend petty concerns and self-interest, and take a vicarious pleasure in training and developing the next generation of managers. But whatever the final attitude toward succession, planned or unplanned, the key players all have to cope with a number of psychological forces that, if not carefully managed, can play havoc with the succession process. And the retiring CEO, who is the central figure in this drama, is particularly susceptible. In the light of these psychological forces, the clinical psychologist and management theorist Harry Levinson has cautioned against CEOs choosing their own successor. He believes that more often than not, CEOs sabotage the process and choose badly.

What makes succession such a sensitive issue? What are the psychological forces we are up against? How does the F-dimension get into the picture? What critical decisions have to be made? How can we facilitate the process? What role can the board and other stakeholders play in these matters?

169

CHAPTER 8

UNCONSCIOUS SABOTAGE

In answering these questions, let's keep in mind that the lack of constructive action on the part of some leaders concerning succession is not necessarily a conscious process. In those instances where succession is fraught with problems, leaders may not even be aware of the exact reasons why they are acting the way they are.

The Denial of Death

The late chancellor of West Germany Konrad Adenauer once asked one of his grandchildren what he wanted to be when he grew up. The little boy replied, "A chancellor like you," to which Adenauer reacted by saying, "That's impossible—there can't be two of us!"

Humorous as the story may appear, it contains a very basic underlying theme. At the heart of the matter is our deep-seated wish to believe in our own immortality. In spite of the forces of reality, psychologically it is very difficult to comprehend and accept the possibility of one's own death. As Freud very astutely put it, "It is indeed impossible to imagine our own death; and whenever we attempt to do so we can perceive that we are in fact still present as spectators. . . . At the bottom no one believes in his own death, or to put the same thing in another way, . . . in the unconscious every one of us is convinced of his own immortality."

Leaders are no exception here. Thinking about succession, let alone actually planning it, brings up the painful, preferably forgotten subject of one's own mortality. And reluctance to deal with the topic is contagious. If senior

170

executives and board members become aware that succession is a sensitive topic to their CEO, they may oblige by avoiding the issue themselves. Talking about succession may be interpreted as a hostile act, as evincing a none-too-subtle desire for the leader's demise. Consciously or unconsciously, retaliation will be feared. It is no wonder that in certain situations every excuse is used to prevent this topic from coming to the fore. Thus, some CEOs continue to act as if death does not exist, and their employees concur. This is particularly the case with founder-managers who tend to have an additional emotional investment in the enterprise since it is a symbol of their success and may have become an extension of their own personality.

In one case, the founder-president of a publishing company refused to accept his own physical decline. In spite of his having had a minor stroke, talk about his condition and the need for a possible successor remained taboo in the company. Senior executives and board members didn't dare to bring up the matter, fearful of his violent temper. Complicating the situation was the fact that the board was made up of old friends, very loyal to the old man, who were unwilling to tackle this problem. Eventually, when a second stroke incapacitated the president, nobody in the company was prepared to step into his shoes. After a lengthy period of upheaval resulting in serious financial losses, the company was acquired by a competitor at a sellout price.

The Legacy

Another possible explanation for this CEO's refusal to deal with succession may have had to do with a deep-seated wish to leave a legacy. One obvious way of coping with the denial of death and the wish for immortality is to leave something tangible behind, a reminder of one's accomplishments while in power. This legacy can take many forms, from physical structures such as an office building or a factory to those intangibles of corporate culture such as a specific management philosophy, an idiosyncratic interpretation of organizational policy, or a particular way of doing things in the organization. When the time comes to hand over power, the outgoing leader may worry about whether a successor will respect the legacy or destroy what has been painstakingly built up over the years. Can he or she be trusted when in power to continue past practices (however inappropriate these may be, given the company's changing environment)? One can never be sure. It is no wonder that leaders are reluctant to let go, and even if they have to, may secretly nourish the hope that their successor will fail. Failure will be considered a further proof of their own indispensability. Thus, they may even take steps, if only subconsciously, to set the successor up for failure.

After a lot of hesitation, the CEO of a large consumer product company finally made the decision to make one of his group vice-presidents the chief operating officer. Soon after his appointment the latter began to take a more active, visible role in the company. From his actions it became clear that the two senior executives had some fundamental differences in management philosophy. Although the CEO tried to accept this, it became an increasing source of irritation to him. Eventually the CEO gave his designated successor an assignment that even under the best of circumstances would have been difficult to handle. To aggravate the situation, a slump occurred in that segment of the industry. Very soon the COO was spending all his time at this division to prevent the situation from worsening. A quick turnaround seemed to be out of the question. The COO's lack of success in solving an impossible situation gave the CEO a handle to convince the board that the former was not the right person for the job, and resulted in a request for his resignation.

Some leaders handle the need for a legacy differently. They try to replicate themselves, looking for successors who are very much like them, people who will carry on in exactly the same way. But frequently this search for clones carries the seeds of failure. What is right for the present may not be the correct course of action, given the needs of the company in the future.

The Illusion of Equality

As I explained in a previous chapter, the ties that bind leader and followers are based on a process of mutual identification. Followers identify with their leaders, and project their ideas onto them; at the same time, they identify with each other. This mutual identification process with the leader and among the followers is what creates a group. It brings about a feeling of unity and belonging and makes for a sense of direction, purpose, and motivation. The precondition for the successful operation of this mutual identification process is the illusion that the leader hands his or her favors out equally and "loves" everyone the same way. Some leaders find it important to maintain this illusion. To single someone out as successor may shatter the sense of togetherness and break the spell. A corollary benefit of not selecting a successor is that this avoids the possibility of guilt feelings about favoritism. If no action is taken and the status quo maintained, the leader does not have to make what might be painful personnel decisions. He does not have to deal with the anger and disappointment of the candidates not chosen.

In one instance, the CEO of an electronics firm had surrounded himself with a group of executives of very uneven talents. Although it was easy to spot the stars, the CEO was unwilling or unable to make the appropriate gestures and reward them accordingly. He would smooth over the mistakes of the more incompetent ones and not praise the high performers for excellence. The perceived unfairness of his treatment became such a bone of contention that eventually a number of his best people left the company. Why this happened, however, remained a puzzle to the CEO. He couldn't understand why people were so upset: as far as he was concerned he had acted correctly by treating everyone equally.

Again, we have to remember that what we are observing is not necessarily a conscious process. This CEO probably had everyone's best interests at heart. But his lack of understanding about his actions eventually backfired.

The King Lear Syndrome

Another contributing factor making for unconscious or even conscious sabotage of the succession process can be called the King Lear syndrome. This name derives from the Shakespeare play one of whose major themes is a warning about the dangers of letting go of power. In the play, the decision to retire and divide his kingdom has devastating consequences for King Lear.

In organizational life this concern is all too real. The economics of power and the knowledge that it is a scarce commodity are ever-present realities. Loyalties shift quickly if it is known that a new person will be taking the reins. Subtle changes begin to occur in relationships. New power networks are created. When this occurs it may be difficult for the outgoing leader to accept a change in power base. What originally may have been a favorable attitude toward the crown prince may turn into resentment. Dormant rivalry may come to the fore and be acted out. Thus to some, having a successor is like signing one's own death warrant!

Peter Lawrence, the very successful CEO of a chain of supermarkets, seemed to do everything right. Realizing that he was getting on in age he personally recruited Fred Pine to head one of the company's major divisions, seeing him as the logical person to lead the company into the next decade. Everyone commended him for his foresight. Not very long after Fred's appointment it became clear that his management style contrasted sharply with that of the CEO. He dominated the operations committee meetings and was responsible for far-reaching alterations in the company's fabric, making it a much leaner operation, with impressive performance implications. Productivity and profits soared. In spite of the excellent results, however, Peter became increasingly annoyed because Fred was receiving most of the credit for the resurgence of the company. Moreover, Fred was not very subtle about his desire to take over Peter's job. Eventually, the two men became engaged in a tug-of-war for control of the company. After a considerable amount of arm twisting, Peter managed to persuade the board that, after all, Fred was not the right person to run

175

the company. He argued that the latter was destroying a corporate culture that had been painstakingly built up over the years and had been a source of major strength to the company. He cited as proof the fact that a number of executives had quit after Fred's arrival. Fred was asked to resign.

Leaders are very familiar with the corridors of power, this being one of the ingredients of their successful rise to the top. Consciously or unconsciously they may resist being treated like a has-been, and often find it difficult to accept their change in status graciously. In fact, they are often extremely unwilling to let go of the reins and, as we saw in the previous example, they may even reconsider their decision to step down. Articles in the popular business press are full of examples of such second thoughts.

To have to work with an officially designated successor is too difficult a task for some leaders. They much prefer to keep the situation ambiguous and maintain their power base. A symptom of this is a rapid succession of crown princes in an organization. William Paley of CBS, Peter Grace of W. R. Grace, and Armand Hammer of Occidental Petroleum are legendary examples of people who tenaciously held or are holding on to power.

From our discussion it becomes clear that these psychodynamic processes can be a serious obstacle to a smooth succession process. When we hear CEOs commenting that they have no time to train a successor, or that, in spite of overwhelming evidence to the contrary, the succession problem has been taken care of, we can be sure that these psychological forces are at work. Once more we can see the obstinate survival of the F-dimension. The same may be said for the CEO who claims that there is no one with the needed qualifications in the company and that suitable people are very hard to find, or that senior managers need more seasoning, or when we find drawn-out, pseudoscientific selection methods as with the Bohlton Company. Such comments and ways of behaving are frequently merely rationalizations covering up a reluctance to let go. Having someone waiting in the wings is too tough an assignment for some CEOs.

WHOM TO CHOOSE

When finally a succession decision has to be made, a very important question is whether the successor should be an insider or an outsider. Which is the better choice? And what are the ramifications of each choice? Unfortunately, research on succession does not provide any clear answers. An understanding of some of the organizational and psychological forces at work, however, may give greater clarity to the matter, particularly in light of the previous discussion.

The Insider

In looking at the insider/outsider choice, we should not discount the effect of existing traditions in a company. Although the succession decision, like most events in organizations, is not exactly a democratic process, it can take place fairly smoothly. In some companies, particularly the larger ones, a good opportunity exists for training and developing successors. In these instances, senior executives aided by the board work out who should be the key contenders. They pick the person most suitable, taking the future needs of the company into consideration. Such a relatively orderly and planned process has obvious advantages. Since the process is spread out over time, it is easier for those not chosen to cope with their disappointment, and this in turn lessens the likelihood of noncooperation later on.

The political forces inside a company tend to favor the selection of an insider. The internal structure of large corporations can be very complex, making it difficult to break up existing coalitions. If an insider is chosen, it is more likely than not that the organization is opting for a maintenance strategy. Loyalty may have been rewarded over organizational change. An obvious advantage is attached to this choice: in general, less turmoil will ensue. Inside choices tend to be less disruptive. With an insider there will be less need to build a new executive team.

On occasion, however, the promotion of an internal candidate can cause problems. It may disrupt the internal pecking order by favoring one organizational unit over another. Thus, sometimes the absence of a neutral point of entry may lead to instability and conflict.

The insider/outsider choice is usually very much determined by self-interest. High-ranking corporate officers and even board members may lobby to influence the decision and may even want the position themselves. These executives know that an inside appointment will make it less likely that they will be replaced. Compromise, the containment of group conflict, and the maintenance of the informal social network may be their prime concerns. But whether this preoccupation with stability and conservation is the wisest choice depends on what is happening in the company's environment.

In one instance—that of a company that had been stagnating for some time—it became obvious that a radically different stance was needed. The company's principal market segment was undergoing rapid changes. In spite of this dangerous situation, which was aggravated by inroads made by competitors, a number of senior managers convinced the board to appoint the executive vice-president as the new CEO. Although the latter was a competent production and operations manager, it was obvious that he lacked the critical skills in marketing and sales that were needed in the company at this time. A number of board members were well aware of this, but they preferred to play it safe and confirm the executive as CEO. The results were devastating, necessitating his replacement soon afterward.

The Outsider

The choice of an outsider often represents a wish within the company for radical change. The conditions have to be right, however, to make this happen. Not surprisingly, a higher incidence of outside successors occurs in failing firms. In these instances, pressure from other constituencies such as the government, banks, and shareholders may have become so strong that the wish of some insiders not to rock the boat may have been overturned.

Outside choices are more likely the longer the tenure of the predecessor. The lengthy occupancy of a position by a leader is frequently a good indication that the individual in question is unwilling to consider a replacement.

A common scenario that then follows is that eventually because of extensive procrastination about the succession decision, the situation inside the company reaches the kind of crisis proportions I mentioned earlier. Consequently, an individual with turnaround skills is needed. Reaching such a situation, particularly in a large company, may be seen as an admission of failure in developing crown princes. In such cases the company can expect a prolonged period of turmoil.

When Tom Lang took command of the financially battered Concorde Corporation he tightened up the bank's lending policies and imposed stringent controls to improve the quality of loans, which had gotten out of hand in the go-go period of his predecessor. Tom's way of managing the bank led to impressive results, but in the process Concorde lost hundreds of executives. Tom certainly didn't feel bound by social obligations; nor did he mind acting as a hatchet man. In this case, in their wish for radical change, the board felt that it had gotten more than it had asked for. Tom's abrasive style, his rigidity, and his obsessiveness in upgrading loan quality led to the loss of a number of important customers. This, combined with the resentment of some of the surviving senior managers, became the basis for his eventual removal.

Tom Lang is an extreme example. Often the presence of an outsider, because of his or her initial position of neutrality, may reduce the likelihood of conflict between departmental subunits during and after the selection process. Also, if a shift in company policy or a major transition program is what is needed, an outsider can afford to be more hard-nosed and act as a hatchet man. In general, outsiders are freer in their actions. It is easier for them to make reassignments and replacements. An outsider is less bound by social obligations, therefore more willing to replace members of the old guard. Most newcomers like to establish their own trusted inner circle of individuals who will be committed to their view of the organization. These strategic changes empower the successor to form a new informal social unit.

The disadvantages that an outsider faces are obvious. It is more difficult for him or her to understand and deal with existing internal power structures. He or she has no informal contacts to rely on. Much time and effort may be needed to break up or cope with hostile coalitions. No wholehearted cooperation can be expected from the old lieutenants who are still licking their wounds at being passed over. The complexities of the organization and the many vested interests can deflect any intended change effort; the entrenchment of established interests is a strong opposing force.

WATCHING THE TRANSITION

What happens when a successor is finally put into place? What are the possible outcomes? What should one be alert for?

Romancing the Past

The obstacles for a new company leader can be formidable. Not only is he or she up against the actual problems existing in the organization, but also, again, a number of intrapsychic forces must be considered. Among them a major one is our tendency to idealize the past. To avoid depression we are all inclined to screen out painful, anxiety-provoking thoughts or events. Pleasant memories often function as a shield to conceal a related painful memory. Some kind of struggle seems to take place psychologically between the defensive process of denial and the forces of memory. Industrial sociologist Alvin Gouldner called this phenomenon the Rebecca Myth: he was referring to the Daphne DuMaurier novel about a young woman who marries a widower and is haunted by people's idealized memories of his first wife, whose virtues are continuously extolled. Dealing psychologically with an absent person can be a formidable task. It is much easier to deal with someone who is present. Interaction with a real person allows for reality testing; with an absent person any fantasy goes.

A strong conservative force influences our behavior. Apprehension and wariness of the new are often apparent. Shakespeare's words about the undiscovered country that "makes us rather bear those ills we have, than fly to others that we know not of" are all too appropriate. We like to hang on to the familiar. And this may have repercussions on the succession process. One of the implications of the Rebecca Myth is that executives in a company and members of the board may block out the excesses of the old CEO's regime and, ignoring reality, hang on to the illusion of how much better things were previously. The successor is in for an uphill battle if he or she wants to overcome this handicap.

Paradise Lost

Even in the case of well-planned successions, some kind of crisis atmosphere is inevitable. Too many changes must be gotten used to and ambiguities sorted out. It is no wonder that we find an increase in dependency reactions among the organization's members in such situations. This makes the symbolic role of the leader even more important. Because of all the uncertainties, many express the desire for someone to give direction and leadership. This tendency to idealize puts enormous psychological pressure on the new leader. It is difficult to handle one's sudden transformation into some kind of messiah, a person who is expected to solve all problems. Expectations may be excessively high. Unfortunately, not many leaders can live up to these ideals of perfection. Otto Kernberg, talking about group processes, mentions in this context that "the 'dependency' group perceive the leader as omnipotent and omniscient and themselves as inadequate, immature, and incompetent. The idealization of the leader is matched by desperate efforts to extract knowledge, power, and goodness from him in a greedy and forever-dissatisfied way. When the leader fails to live up to such an ideal of perfection, the members react first with denial and then with a rapid complete devaluation of him and a search for substitute leadership."

This human characteristic explains why leaders tend to have more influence during crisis than during noncrisis periods. As I have mentioned before, a crisis is a time of increased dependency reactions. The positive side of this psychological process in action in the case of succession is that it makes for an initial honeymoon period when the leader receives enthusiasm and commitment. Some leaders take advantage of the momentum thus created to very good effect. Given this process of great expectations, the new leader seems to be most influential just before taking charge.

But how long can the honeymoon last? Most leaders are only mortal and find it hard to meet all these exaggerated expectations. The outcome is predictable: a shift in emotional attitudes toward the new leader occurs. What once was idealization or infatuation quickly turns into disillusion born of anger at being disappointed—at the leader's failing to live up to the ideals of perfection. And those who have been passed by for the position may now be the ones responsible for orchestrating this mood swing. They may initiate the rebellion, acting out their lingering resentment. Thus, the new leader is rapidly devalued and turns from the long-awaited messiah into a scapegoat who is blamed for all the company's problems, past and present. Paradoxically, usually at the same time, the regime of the predecessor is glorified.

THE ROLE OF THE BOARD

At times of succession, the strongest countervailing force that can be used to bring greater reality to the CEO is usually the board. Other possible agents are shareholders and banks, but since the board ultimately has to approve the choice of successor, it has the greatest scope to influence events. It is therefore worthwhile to take a brief look at the way in which board members can help smooth out the process and choose an effective new leader. First, it seems obvious that the CEO should not be the only person involved in the selection process. Instead, the board should take a very active stand. If it does not, given the psychological forces at work, the possibility exists that the succession decision may be endlessly postponed or carried out in such a way that the successor is likely to fail.

The board should also play a key role in deciding whether an insider or an outsider is the right choice. If planned well, inside succession gives fewer surprises and is less disturbing to an organization. Unfortunately, planning for orderly management succession is not as common as it should be, particularly given the all-too-human tendency to be very sensitive to the faults of insiders and stress their weaknesses but take their virtues for granted. Thus, even if capable insiders are around they may not be chosen.

Given the potential for problems during the transition period, the board should also be particularly vigilant at the beginning of the tenure of a new CEO. This is usually the period when the new CEO needs most help. The board can be particularly helpful in managing the disappointment of those key contenders not chosen for the outgoing CEO's job. In those instances where future collaboration seems impossible, they can play a role in facilitating these individuals' exit and help the new CEO manage the process. The board should also not hesitate to intervene if mistakes are made by the new CEO. It is not a good idea to let mistakes fester so that more draconian decisions have to be taken later on. The transition period is a time when the board has extraordinary power to shape the future of the company.

Too many boards, unfortunately, are too ossified, incestuous, or dependent to play this monitoring role successfully. Frequently, partisan politics sways effective decision making with dire consequences for the company. But this may be changing. The more recent development by which greater accountability is legally required from members of the board is a step in the right direction. Unfortunately, the threat of litigation has also caused some more capable executives to think twice before joining a board. A truly effective board, however, can play an active role in imaginative decision making and can also serve as some kind of personal counselor to outgoing and incoming leaders to help them work through the transition process.

One question remains: What qualities should we look for when we are recruiting a new leader? What characteristics serve as an antidote against the F-dimension? What makes a really great organizational leader? Much has already been written on this subject and, at the risk of adding to the existing confusion, I will try to give some pointers in the next chapter.

9

"I'd Follow That Man—Anywhere—Blindfolded": Effective Leadership

He was a great thundering paradox of a man, noble and ignoble, inspiring and outrageous, arrogant and shy, the best of men and the worst of men, the most protean, most ridiculous, and most sublime. No more baffling, exasperating soldier ever wore a uniform. Flamboyant, imperious, and apocalyptic, he carried the plumage of a flamingo, could not acknowledge errors, and tried to cover up his mistakes with sly, childish tricks. Yet he was also endowed with great personal charm, a will of iron, and a soaring intellect. Unquestionably he was the most gifted man-at-arms this nation has produced.

William Manchester, *American Caesar*

T hus reads the opening paragraph of William Manchester's biography of General Douglas MacArthur. In this passage the enigmatic qualities of his personality are well captured. Manchester describes a person who is different, a giant of a man, not easily disregarded. We find ourselves face to face with someone who knows the ins and outs of the influence game. This leader looms larger than life. It is hard to remain indifferent to him. Those who knew him either admired or disliked him. Whatever reservations we may have about MacArthur's behavior, about his exhibitionism, his haughtiness, or his inconsistencies, we cannot doubt his leadership qualities. As one of his officers said, "I'd follow that man—anywhere—blindfolded."

MacArthur, like De Benedetti and Richard Branson, is an unusual example of a highly effective leader. These men illustrate how leaders can make a difference and function well in spite of all the regressive forces I have described. After our discussion of some of the darker sides of leadership, such leaders, given their efficacy, offer the opportunity to look at the other side of the coin. What distinguishes these leaders? What makes them so effective? What quali-

189

ties enable them to uplift their followers? How do they cope successfully with the F-dimension?

Any assessment of the qualities of effective leadership is difficult because of the interaction of three sets of variables. As my discussion has made obvious, leadership is not only a function of the leader but also of the complex interaction of leader, followers, and the historical moment in which they are operating. While I do, of course, recognize the importance of leader–follower interaction and its context, here I will concentrate on leadership characteristics.

In taking this approach it is difficult to avoid coming up with a shopping list of qualities. Obviously, any leader is unlikely to possess them all, and is likely to possess particular qualities in different combinations. Since the list is by no means exhaustive, leaders may possess other qualities as well.

As I have done throughout this book, I will deal with both surface and deep qualities—those that appeal to the rational abilities of the followers and those that strike directly at the unconscious. Clearly, one cannot understand leadership without paying attention to the psychodynamic aspects, to those elements that make for the F-dimension. I will also examine how the surface and deep psychological structures affect leaders themselves, since how leaders transform images of power in their inner theater eventually determines the overall efficacy of their actions.

QUALITIES OF EFFECTIVE LEADERS

A few decades ago, Charles de Gaulle, a great leader himself, wrote, "There can be no prestige without mystery, for familiarity breeds contempt. . . . In the designs, the demeanor, and the mental operations of a leader there must be always a 'something' which others cannot altogether fathom, which puzzles them, stirs them, and rivets their attention . . . . If one is to influence men's minds, one must observe them carefully and make it clear that each has been marked out from among his fellows. . . .

"This attitude of reserve demands, as a rule, a corresponding economy of words and gestures. . . . There would even seem to be some relationship between a man's inner force and his outward seeming. . . . The great leaders have always carefully stage-managed their effects."

In the same vein, de Gaulle lists as other characteristics of leadership "a readiness to launch great undertakings and a determination to see things through to the end." He adds that the leader "must aim high, show that he has vision, act on the grand scale." And he continues by saying that the effective leader needs to be well informed of the details of specific situations and not only think in abstractions or vague, generalized theories. He adds that a leader "must outbid his rivals in self-confidence."

Charles de Gaulle knew what he was talking about. He had ample opportunity to test his ideas. His concept of leadership did not permit mediocrity: it was of a grandiose nature. He could appropriately have been described as charismatic. He was one of those leaders who holds a spellbinding power over his or her followers, the type of person who becomes a transforming agent able to shape and alter and elevate the motives and values and goals of followers.

De Gaulle derived his experience from taking on the role of France's guide and head of state. Many years of training as a soldier and resistance fighter went to prepare him for this role. And when the opportunity eventually came, he rose to the occasion. De Gaulle was a master in the influence game. He knew how to sustain his power base through direct, dramatic appeals to the people. Crisis management, as during the Algerian situation, was his forte. In spite of the damage to French self-esteem that the loss of this long-cherished dominion entailed, de Gaulle was able to unite the nation behind him. He knew how to balance *action* and *reflection*. He never was a mere pawn of external pressures. He would draw strength from his inner images to sustain his actions. He would not fall back into a mere reactive mode. Moreover, his style, his skills in stagecraft, and his radiation of self-confidence during appearances made many of his otherwise highly unpopular actions palatable.

When we analyze his statements carefully we can discern a number of themes that are echoed by other leaders in action.

The Dream

As de Gaulle indicated, effective leaders are propelled by a vision. They have a view of the future that becomes highly compelling to others. As a good example we can take Franklin Delano Roosevelt's concept of the New Deal, which became his way to fight the Great Depression. Hitler had a demonic vision of a new Germany as described in his book *Mein Kampf*, where he predicts the coming of the Thousand Year Reich. Gandhi imagined an India, freed from the British, where Hindus and Moslems would live in harmony. Martin Luther King Jr.'s dream of harmony between blacks and whites was of a similar visionary nature. In describing their dreams, leaders often use the imagery of a journey: a path to follow, or being at a crossroad.

We can see how these magnificent obsessions create a focus and a sense of direction, thereby mobilizing followers to pursue a course of action to its successful conclusion. What seems to happen is that leaders create a shared vision of the future. They seem to be able to mold existing images in their internal, private world in such a way that these become acceptable on an external, public stage. Moreover, these people seem to differ from others in that they possess starkly pronounced internal scenarios, mental codes for representing experiences that guide their behavior. And as I have indicated in my descriptions of leadership styles, these scenarios can be positive, implying that these are based on a cohesive, well-integrated sense of self, or negative, in which case they may be a reactive, compensatory way of dealing with perceived hurts and insecurity. These scenarios are transmitted to the followers in such a way that they create a shared reality. And we are now familiar with the mechanisms by which followers project their fantasies on leaders. Hence, these inner scenarios become the "sustaining myth," or set of myths, which gives the people composing the societies a sense of what it means to be a member of them. Eventually they become the building blocks for action.

General Douglas MacArthur is a good example of an individual whose inner scenario was constructive and relatively benign. Reading his *Reminiscences*, we realize the extent to which his internal world was populated with the heroic images of his grandfather, father, and older brother. His life's task became to emulate a father described by his comrades-in-arms as "magnificent . . . afraid of nothing . . . [a man] who would fight a pack of tigers in a jungle . . . the hero of the regiment." Such exalted imagery was combined with the confidence created by a mother who would tell him, "You'll win if you don't lose your nerve. You must believe in yourself . . . or no one else will believe in you. Be self-confident, self-reliant, and even if you don't make it, you will know you have done your best." With such a support system of reliable, dependable figures incorporated in his inner world, no wonder MacArthur became the leader he was. Moreover, and not surprisingly in the light of his specific background, part of his destiny was to return and be the liberator of the Philippines, a country that his father had once ruled as governor-general, from its Japanese invaders.

In the business realm, we can observe similar processes at work. For example, we have seen how the first Henry Ford foresaw a cheap car for the masses at a time when automobiles were becoming more and more luxurious and expensive. As indicated before, his major preoccupation was a dream to ease the life of the farmer, which for its part, we might infer, was based on an ambivalent attitude toward a special farmer, his father.

Another example of externalizing internal conflict can be found in the life of Walt Disney, who had a dream of family togetherness through wholesome entertainment. Again, in his case, the source of his preoccupation is not difficult to infer given his particular background. His dream represented the realization of a wish rarely fulfilled in his own home environment. Although his mother seems to have been a kindhearted woman during his childhood, she was not strong enough to stand up to his father, an

194

extremely forbidding, stern, highly religious man who never laughed or played with his children, and who had absolutely no sense of fun, but only disapproved. Maybe there were many good reasons for this attitude. Hard times because of farm failures, financial problems, illness, and social and geographical uprooting may have contributed to his father's bad temper. Adding to Walt Disney's longing for family togetherness may have been his lonely position in the family, his brothers being much older and his sister much younger than he. Another indication of family unhappiness was the fact that quarrels about feeling exploited by their father eventually caused all three older brothers to run away from home. Perhaps one of the few happy moments of Walt Disney's childhood was a short period on his father's farm, a time during which he observed and played with wild and domestic animals and learned how to draw. A rabbit and a pig became his first drawings; these were later to be used in his cartoons.

Management of Meaning

An essential part of effective leadership is managing meaning. Leaders need to articulate their dreams and make these attractive to their followers. They do this using language, ceremonies, symbols, and settings. Historical and mythological figures are also evoked and emulated, tapping cultural roots; these are all strategic maneuvers to mobilize support. Here leadership and stagecraft join forces. Effective leaders emanate theater. They possess great oratorical skills and know how to make use of humor, irony, and the colloquial. They seem to know how to talk directly to their followers' unconscious, employing figurative language such as similes and metaphors to facilitate identification by their followers. Moreover, in presenting their ideas their sense of timing often seems uncanny and is a key factor in making their actions so effective. They are masters in the creation of suspense.

The unsettling emotional nature of these symbolic methods of communication makes for their spellbinding quality and induces the potentially dangerous reactions of dependency, regression, and transference. Indeed, Freud compared the peculiar psychological relationship between leaders and followers with that of a hypnotist and his subject. As I have indicated already, leaders, in one way or another, create in their followers a desire to be taken care of. And given the expectations leaders raise, they seem to be the logical figures to do the caretaking. Idealization of the leader by his or her followers is part of this process. Leaders reawaken past relationships of dominance and submission and revive earlier dependency relationships. As we have seen in the discussion on transference, significant individuals from childhood become intertwined with contemporary figures. The leader becomes the depository of the followers' fantasies. And even incompetents have the benefit of the doubt and profit from this psychological process. Thus, to some extent, each leader becomes a product of our own fantasies.

Effective leaders are masters in the manipulation of meaning. Part of this process entails scapegoating: splitting the world into us versus them or good versus bad becomes a familiar pattern. In such a dialogue, simplification, stark contrast, and extremes become the rule; dramatization and histrionics are essential. To make this happen, truly effective leaders know how to use simple language, which makes their message come across easily. Personal fears, aggression, and aspirations are projected onto social causes that allow for symbolic solutions. This regressive process of externalization may result in a release of tension. Freud, following le Bon, a French student of group behavior, said, "A group is extraordinarily credulous and open to influence, it has no critical faculty, and the improbable does not exist for it. It thinks in images, which call one another up by association (just as they arise with individuals in states of free imagination), and whose agreement with reality is never checked by any reasonable agency. The feelings of a group are always very simple and very exaggerated. So a group knows neither doubt nor uncertainty."

With this knowledge of the regressive potential of group processes in mind, we can see how a political leader like Winston Churchill could engage in high drama and stir his audience by saying to those who joined him in his fight against Hitler, "I have nothing to offer but blood, toil, tears, and sweat." Douglas MacArthur vowed "I shall return," making these words to the Filipinos a symbol of victory and freedom, a magical promise that they would be liberated from the Japanese. We recall Franklin Delano Roosevelt's statement "The only thing we have to fear is fear itself." John F. Kennedy stated memorably in his inaugural address, "Ask not what your country can do for you; ask what you can do for your country."

Although on a less grandiose scale, business leaders use comparable imagery. I mentioned in an earlier chapter how the management of meaning is staged at the Mary Kay Cosmetics annual meeting. The message of hardship, hope, and success is clear in this theater piece: the pink Cadillac

197

will be waiting for that heroine who manages to overcome all the hurdles and reach the targeted sales level!

IBM's Thomas Watson Sr. is another example of a real master in the management of meaning. His skill in stagecraft was honed by John Patterson, the business genius behind National Cash Register. After being fired by his mentor, Watson Sr. quickly came into his own, working for CTR (IBM's name at the time). An exceptionally talented salesman, he was a master of using slogans to disseminate his beliefs about respect for the individual employee, the need to give the best customer service in the world, and the imperative to excel in everything. He would say such things as "Time lost is time gone forever"; "There is no such thing as standing still; we must never feel satisfied"; "A team that won't be beat, can't be beat"; "A company is known by the men it keeps"; "You cannot be a success in any business without believing that it is the greatest business in the world"; and "Business is fun." And, of course, his favorite admonition was "Read—Listen—Discuss—Observe—*Think!*"

His speeches became legendary. At sales meetings songs were sung about the chief, adding to the mythmaking process. One song, for example, ended as follows:

> Mr. Watson is the man we're working for,
> He's the leader of the CTR,
> He's the fairest, squarest man we know;
> Sincere and true.
> He has shown us how to play the game
> And how to make the dough.

In training programs, Watson Sr.'s ways of managing meaning became institutionalized. Pictures of him were found throughout the organization. And quoting from his speeches was part of everyday conversation among IBM's high flyers. In managing all this, Watson Sr. was turning his salespeople into a well-trained army. They had to be clean-cut, in good physical shape, conservatively dressed. Liquor was forbidden at IBM functions. Instead of receiving medals, those men or women who had met their quotas became members of the Hundred Percent Club. Everyone knew that a career in sales was the route to the executive suite, but of course, via that club.

Network Building

Effective leaders possess great interpersonal skills. They are master communicators not only on a mass scale but also at a more intimate level. After all, the support of a core group of dedicated followers has helped them to get where they are now. Those who rise to the top are very skilled in influencing, controlling, and manipulating their followers. They seem to be able to deal with emotionally tough situations. They are capable of providing some kind of holding environment, thus managing to contain their followers' emotions.

Effective leaders are very sensitive to other people and can listen and understand others' points of view. As the management theorists McCall and Lombardo discovered in their findings on successful and unsuccessful leaders, "the most frequent cause for derailment [along the path to the executive suite] was insensitivity to other people." In their study, the ineffective leaders turned out to be the ones who were abrasive, intimidating, and unwilling to participate in the give-and-take of the influence game. Instead,

199

their defenses tended to be rigid and they managed their emotions poorly.

Effective leaders are also masters of creating and maintaining organizational networks for interacting with and monitoring the activities of their key subordinates. They are very aware of those on whom they are dependent, and vice versa. They manage their relationships with key subordinates very carefully. Hiring, firing, and promotion are some of the tools they use to maintain their networks. Sophisticated control systems are another way of fostering these interdependencies.

Franklin Delano Roosevelt was a leader talented in handling this particular facet of leadership. His skill in network building and manipulation was legendary. To illustrate, one of the first things he did after taking office was to develop an organizational intelligence system to prevent himself from becoming a captive of the complex official bureaucracy of Washington. A well-known analyst of his presidency, the political scientist Richard Neustadt, recorded, "Not only did he keep his organizations overlapping and divide authority among them, but he also tended to put men of clashing temperaments, outlooks, ideas, in charge of them. Competitive personalities mixed with competing jurisdictions was Roosevelt's formula for putting pressure on himself, for making his subordinates push up to him the choices they could not take for themselves. It also made them advertise their punches; their quarrels provided him with not only heat but information."

One of the master network builders in the business realm has been Alfred P. Sloan, the former president of General Motors. His talent for managing information flows made him one of the fathers of the modern corporation.

Sloan succeeded in consolidating the loosely knit federation of operating enterprises started by William Durand, the founder of General Motors. Sloan's actions transformed General Motors and made it the company it is today. He saw very early the value of general administrative controls and committee structures. His blueprint for change was his "Organization Study," an analysis of General Motors' needs and an attempt at mastering the information flow of the then-tottering giant. His membership in the executive committee, the finance committee, and the various interdivisional relations committees (the latter set up to coordinate decisions relating to purchasing, sales, operations, and technology) put him in the middle of a network of information and kept him closely informed of the modus operandi of staff and general officers of the corporation. And given the financial results at the time, he seems to have put this information to good use.

Pattern Recognition

Studies of effective leaders have repeatedly emphasized their ability to recognize patterns and relationships among seemingly disjointed events. Effective leaders are masters of sense making, of bringing order to the chaos that tends to surround them. They can sort relevant from irrelevant information. They know how to prevent themselves from being swamped by sensory and informational overloads. They are what has been called reducers (as opposed to augmenters), having the ability to limit the amount of stimulation impinging on them. They can tolerate high arousal levels. To use Kipling's words, they keep their heart when all about them are losing theirs. They successfully

201

engage in multiple activities without feeling overcommitted or experiencing a sense of discomfort and exhaustion. This characteristic enables them to deal with complex, novel, and interesting situations without impaired task performance, cognitive disorganization, or health problems.

Through selective combination and selective comparison, effective leaders know how to weave connections. This makes them highly skilled in putting together isolated pieces of information. They possess the ability to manage conceptual complexity. They are flexible in the cognitive differentiation and integration of information, so that they can process data according to the needs of the situation. If simple information processing is required, they reject dissonant information. But if the situation warrants it, effective leaders integrate and combine multiple points of view simultaneously and look for novel solutions.

The CEO of a financial services company demonstrated this talent very clearly. The information flow in this multibusiness, multinational company was phenomenal. The amount of data that ended up on the president's desk seemed to be more than normal mortals would be able to handle. The same could be said about the number of meetings she had to attend given her many different functions. Nevertheless, time after time, she would surprise her subordinates with her ability to tease out the essentials. The key to this information management was her ability to clearly separate tactical (short-term) concerns from strategic (long-term) ones. In all her activities, she kept a set of long-term company objectives in the back of her mind. Given the myriad of other activities she was involved in, her ability to set priorities helped her to keep perspective.

Harold Geneen, the former president and CEO of ITT, also possessed this talent, although given his particular organizational design, what originally may have been a strength seems to have become somewhat perverted. He was the master of the "unshakeable fact": he was skilled at uncovering layers of false "facts" to ferret out the truth. His ability to digest massive amounts of information became legendary. Unfortunately, his hunger for facts turned the company into a paper factory, a place where an inappropriate amount of time was spent in turning out marginally useful information.

Empowerment

Charles de Gaulle once remarked that the real leader should aim high and carefully draw out his followers. Indeed, effective leaders communicate high performance expectations to their followers and show confidence in their ability to meet these expectations. By making their followers feel significant, they manage to motivate them. Their high expectations seem to enhance their followers' sense of self-esteem and feelings of competence, thereby increasing their effectiveness. Effective leaders know how to create commitment. By harnessing the energies of their followers and translating intention into sustained reality, they encourage them to attain unexpected results.

We don't have to look far to find examples in the political sphere of how to motivate followers to transcend their more pedestrian preoccupations. John Kennedy said when he became the Democratic presidential candidate, "We stand today on the edge of a new frontier." Charles de Gaulle expressed the same kind of confidence in his followers when he stated at the beginning of World War II that "France has lost the battle but she has not lost the war." More than a hundred years before him, Napoleon Bonaparte proclaimed confidently that "every French soldier carries in his cartridge-pouch the baton of a marshall of France." What all these leaders had in common was the ability to create an atmosphere of excitement, enthusiasm, and motivation among their followers.

Tracy Kidder describes how a group of computer wizards at Data General was motivated to achieve the impossible. Under the leadership of Tom West, who knew how to produce commitment in the face of impossible odds, they created a new computer, symbolically called "the Eagle," in one year. West's way of inspiring commitment and motivation became the material myth is made of. Kidder quotes one of West's subordinates as follows:

> West's never unprepared in any kind of meeting. He doesn't talk fast or raise his voice. He conveys—it's not enthusiasm exactly, it's the intensity of someone who's weathering a storm and showing us the way out. He's saying, "Look, we gotta move this way." Then once he gets the VPs to say it sounds good, Tom goes to some of the software people and some of his own people. "The bosses are signed up for this," he tells them. "Can I get you signed up to do your part?" He goes around and hits people one at a time, gets 'em enthused. They say, "Ahhh, it sounds like you're just gonna put a bag on the side of the Eclipse" [the name of another computer], and Tom'll give 'em his little grin and say, "It's more than that, we're really gonna build this fucker and it's gonna be fast as greased lightning;" He tells them, "We're gonna do it by

April." That's less than a year away, but never mind. Tom's message is: "Are you guys gonna do it or sit on your ass and complain?" It's a challenge he throws at them. . . . He put new life into a lot of people's jobs.

We see how statements of confidence on a large, rather abstract scale are thus reinforced by more individual, personalized assertions. And given the results, it can be seen that this kind of special treatment has great motivational value.

Competence

Technical skills are listed in *Stogdill's Handbook of Leadership* as a very important factor in effective leadership. We have seen the importance de Gaulle assigned to this aspect of leadership. Leaders need to be familiar with the substance of the matter. They have to know what they are talking about. If they don't, they quickly lose credibility. Thinking in purely abstract terms alone is not good enough. Not only must leaders recognize the big picture, they must also be familiar with the specifics of the situation; this enables them to be realistic in making recommendations. They must therefore have some familiarity with the exact nature of the work to be done.

Chairman Iacocca of the Chrysler Corporation is a good case in point. It goes without saying that his skills in dramatization were essential in saving the ailing corporation. Anyone possessing a television set would agree. Without that skill, he would not have been given financial assistance from the government, received the backing from the unions to accept a pay cut, or persuaded consumers to buy his

205

cars. One other key factor was his intimate familiarity with the ins and outs of the car industry. He knew what it meant to build an automobile. He understood how different segments of the production process interacted. He knew how to use control systems to pull together the disparate fiefdoms that made up Chrysler. It was this specific knowledge that made him so effective when articulating his vision of organizational renewal.

Hardiness and Perseverance

To be a leader requires a certain amount of hardiness. A lot of endurance is needed to cope with the stresses and strains of a rapidly changing environment. Effective leaders know how to manage stress. They possess a positive and stable self-image. They firmly believe that they can control what affects their life. In their behavior they exude a sense of meaningfulness and they interact vigorously with their environment; they are committed to the activities in their lives, and see change as a challenge.

With hardiness comes perseverance. True leaders belong to that group of people who do not easily give up, those who keep on trying and insisting that their demands be met. They stick to their original objective in spite of all difficulties. Their preoccuptions can make them sound at times like a broken record, but they are convinced that such behavior will eventually bear fruit. Furthermore, if so required, these individuals know how to wait. They will bide their time and wait for the right moment. Effective leaders believe firmly in their ideas and are willing to see them through, whatever the setbacks. They keep on asking, talking, explaining. They have incredible staying power; they never let up. Their inner scenario with its magnificent obsession and stark, pronounced imagery keeps them going. They emanate integrity. Moreover, their actions are characterized by a certain amount of consistency, while at the same time they leave space for the unexpected.

Studying the life histories of many entrepreneurs, one finds that perseverance turns up over and over again. The architect of Europe's integration, Jean Monnet, is a good case in point. In his memoirs he wrote, "I am not an optimist. I am simply persistent. If action is necessary, how can one say that it is impossible, so long as one has not tried it? . . . Events that strike me and occupy my thoughts lead me to general conclusions about what has to be done. . . . I can wait a long time for the right moment. In Cognac, they are good at waiting. It is the only way to make good brandy."

Although Walt Disney, the founder of the Disney Corporation, is now a household name and has been hailed as the world's most successful creator of screen animation, success did not come easily to him. Only sheer persistence against sometimes impossible odds enabled him to attain the acclaim he has today. Reading his life history, one can see that every step on the way was an uphill battle: going from black and white to color, putting sound into animation, making a full feature-length film. When he wasn't being taken in by crooks or having his animators raided by other studios, he was being blocked by his brother Roy, the latter being fearful that his ideas were too costly and that they would go broke. His *Snow White* project certainly did not receive a warm reception. It was viewed as being far too costly, although it turned out to be one of the most successful films of all time. The idea of mixing classical music

207

with cartoon accompaniment, which resulted in the film *Fantasia,* didn't have a much better reception and was thought to be nonsensical. His design for a theme park, Disneyland, was rejected as well. Disney was turned down everywhere he went trying to obtain financing for the project. The kind of reception he received made him decide to do it on his own and finance it himself, starting a new company to circumvent the objections of his brother and other shareholders. Not surprisingly, given his persistence, these critics eventually changed their minds.

Enactment

Persistence and hardiness alone are not good enough; these qualities have to be combined with enactment. Many people have lots of ideas, but that is the stage where things usually remain. The idea never progresses to implementation. Effective leaders are different. They go one step further and are the doers, bringing about their own environment; they are proactive. Such people have a great ability to initiate and sustain interaction with others and create the ambiance to make their ideas work. They know how to come up with new ideas and make these viable.

An excellent case in point has been the behavior of Akio Morita, cofounder and chairman of Sony Corporation. What some may derogatorially call Morita's impulsiveness may better be described as an ability to make bold decisions where more traditional executives would hesitate. Morita's involvement in the execution of what originally looked like a crazy idea, the Walkman portable stereo, is only a small example of his contribution to the success of the company.

High achievement motivation, the need to do something better than has been done before, helps trigger enactment. This high need for achievement drives effective leaders and is very characteristic of them. Such individuals strive to make things happen, and have entrepreneurial talents. They are willing to take calculated risks; however, they also recognize when risk taking becomes excessive.

THE ROLE OF THE EFFECTIVE LEADER'S INNER THEATER

Great leaders, then, are characterized by qualities that are both external and rational, on the one hand, and internal and unconscious, on the other. External, rational manifestations include vision, communication and interpersonal skills, information analysis skills, the ability to motivate others, technical competence, hardiness, perseverance, and the ability to carry out ideas. But these surface skills are based on what is happening in the inner theaters of the leader and followers. Thus, the magnificent obsession—the leader's vision—is made compelling to others by the stability or conflict of images in a leader's inner world and the transference reactions affecting followers. If this process occurs at the right moment in the social environment, this interface can become an extremely powerful force. Effective communication of the vision depends in large part on the way leaders appeal to their followers' unconscious, creating in them a desire to be taken care of and a wish to participate in grandiose actions. Even hardiness and perseverance stem from unconscious forces—the positive and stable self-image of the leader—while the ability to get

209

things done seems related to the high achievement motivation produced by forceful inner imagery.

It would be an oversimplification, however, to suggest that the inner images of great leaders are all benign. As we saw in some of our examples, some malevolent core conflictual relationship themes in a leader's inner world can also produce positive results because of the way the individual reacts to them and tries to compensate for them. In fact, coping successfully with such regressive forces is one of the hallmarks of a great leader.

The qualities described in this chapter tend to have a buffering effect against the F-dimension, helping the leader avoid some of the pitfalls of leadership I have described elsewhere in this book. For example, the ability to withstand stress and operate at high arousal levels may carry a leader through times of organizational crisis, enabling him or her to cope with the increased dependency needs of subordinates. Similarly, hardiness and perseverance can help new leaders whose followers' exaggerated expectations turn to sudden devaluation if the leader fails to achieve immediately all that was hoped. Interpersonal and technical skills, and the ability to make sense of large quantities of information, can help keep CEOs in touch with reality, making it less likely that they will be tempted to surround themselves with yes-men, indulge in flights of grandiose fancy, or initiate folie à deux. If a leader has clear vision and the ability to articulate it, the fact that others will come to share it can take away some of the loneliness of command; high achievement motivation can help compensate for this, too, and can help the leader who has to make painful personnel and other decisions.

In general, then, great leaders are those who possess particular qualities at both the surface and the unconscious level, and who succeed in addressing these two levels in their followers. At the same time, they must be strong enough to withstand, both personally and in others, the regressive unconscious forces that their leadership position arouses.

10
The Leader as Symbol

Yatha Raja, tatha praja.
(As the king is, so are the people.)
Hindu Proverb

*It is a true proverb, that if you live
with a lame man you will learn to limp.*
Plutarch, *Morals*

A man who is very busy seldom changes his opinions.
Nietzsche, *Human All-Too-Human*

J ean Riboud, the late CEO of
Schlumberger, was not your
typical businessman. Yet his multinational oil field service
company, doing business in ninety-two countries, was
hailed by Wall Street during the reign of this "quiet giant"
as one of the best-managed companies in the world. He was
in fact a model transformational business leader, helping
people believe in something larger than themselves, but was
also described as someone impersonating a businessman,
someone "who is trying to hide a certain poetry." Riboud
was a man of contrasts, a very successful capitalist who
called himself a socialist; immersed in business but having a deep love for the arts, literature, and politics; tough-
minded but also generous and modest; charming and committed but at the same time reserved and distant. Riboud
was a business leader in whom that rare combination of
action and reflection could be seen. And his record was en-
viable. During his two decades in power, Schlumberger's
revenue grew twenty times, net income multiplied forty-
four times, and stock value increased thirty-five times. That
is not to say that Riboud was the perfect manager; far from
that. To some extent he was fortunate in that his period in

215

power coincided with the oil boom. And certainly there was room for improvement in some of his interpersonal relations. For example, he was capable of holding long grudges. In fact, some people compared him to an elephant, a person who would not forget: when he felt wronged he excluded those who had wronged him, even if they were friends and family members, from his personal sphere. He also made mistakes in business. Some of his acquisitions have been seriously questioned and were abandoned after his death. Moreover, his way of running the corporation, reallocating people frequently, could take a heavy toll on personal life. And some of the things he preached, he didn't apply to himself, the succession question being a good example. However, on balance, he must be seen as a great leader.

One of Riboud's preoccupations in running Schlumberger was his fear that it would lose its entrepreneurial flair—that built-in conservative forces would take over, making the company too complacent. To fight this tendency and give people in his organization new challenges and new motivation, he was a master of the unexpected. "Permanent cultural revolution" was his motto, and became a way of life under his reign. Although people mattered to him, the welfare of the company came first. He said, "If you want to be St. Francis of Assisi, you should not head a public company." He would give as the reason for Schlumberger's success "the will to win," the essence of the company's spirit. He would say, "It's easy to be the best, but that's not enough. The goal is to strive for perfection." At the same time, however, he did not want his employees to steamroller those they dealt with, to be too aggressive.

To instill his management philosophy, he would spend an extraordinary amount of time on people issues, selecting individuals who could think for themselves. As he said himself, "The only seat belt I know in business turbulence is to determine for oneself a few convictions, a few guidelines, and to stick by them." He didn't want his people to follow fashions and become part of the establishment, "to float like a cork." He said, "Profit should not be the only element in judging human life." In his mind, the corporation had to take on some of the responsibilities that religion used to have in the past.

Jean Riboud combined many of the positive leadership qualities that I discussed in the previous chapter. Such qualities can help combat the regressive forces that are so often brought to bear on leaders. As we can see from the case of Riboud, perhaps the greatest strength leaders can have to help them deal with these forces is the ability not only to act but also to *reflect* on their actions. If leaders are unable to step back and examine the consequences of their behavior, regressive forces may come to the fore, the hazards of a specific leadership style may become too pronounced, or leaders may create closed communities, losing touch with reality.

We have seen in earlier chapters of this book how frequently many of these regressive forces can be brought to bear simultaneously. Leaders who do not recognize them and are unable to withstand them are the ones who cannot manage. Such leaders are swept away by paranoia and depression, the real banes of leadership. We should not forget that these regressive forces are ever present. Leaders should be aware of this and should be able to identify

217

potential signs of trouble and take preventive action. They should not forget that the ability to change fantasy into reality, given their power, is like a siren's call and may cause a metamorphosis as soon as an individual attains a position of leadership. The potential for irrational behavior is dormant in each of us.

Fortunately, as in the case of Riboud, many leaders have sufficient strength of character and adequate coping abilities to prevent this from happening: they have the inner resources and characteristics to manage the new pressures that leadership brings. Such leaders are willing to test and reevaluate reality and to periodically reappraise their own values, actions, and interpersonal relationships.

Corrective action and change derive from the ability to realize when certain actions are becoming destructive and why the F-dimension exists. Successful leaders who have the courage to look at their own blind spots are willing to ask for professional guidance if needed.

In the end, it is these executives who possess real freedom of choice, acting out of an inner sense of security instead of being merely impulse-driven. Self-examination enhances a person's identity, strengthens reality testing, fosters adaptation to change, and limits susceptibility to controlling influences. Because these qualities form the basis for mature working relationships, mutual reality-oriented problem solving, and a healthy organizational culture, self-examination can deter regression in organizational leadership.

As well as these inner safeguards, several external ones may help prevent the emergence of potential leadership pitfalls. Of course, compared to some political leaders, business leaders are comparatively restricted in their actions, and it is thus usually somewhat easier to set up safeguards against excess. The government or unions may take on the role of countervailing power, for example. Moreover, in many large bureaucratic organizations with committee structures, checks and balances exist in the form of distribution of key policy decisions over a number of individuals and agencies. Also, organizational processes tend to maintain their own momentum, and are resistant to dramatic change. Large organizations often have a high degree of inertia. Social systems have their own way of providing a safety belt for individuals through their structure. From an organizational perspective, a number of steps can be taken to influence the nature of strategic decision making and the degree of corporate slack. These can include innovative human resource management policies and design of flatter, more participative organizations. All of these interventions can have a balancing effect.

Another very important countervailing power to prevent regressive forces from coming to the fore can be the feedback of outsiders: such people as external directors, bankers, and consultants. Individuals from outside the organization usually possess a very different frame of reference and are much less entangled and blinded by the existing organizational dynamics. They can provide more of an overall view and warn of potential sources of trouble. Of course, this is only possible if the leader is sufficiently attached to reality to listen to them.

Top executive training programs are another potential countervailing force worth mentioning. Such programs can provide a nonthreatening environment where senior executives can discuss their working experience with colleagues and professionals exposed to similar problems. These situations, again, may have a beneficial effect on reality testing. Mutual comparison of potential problem areas may provide these leaders with an "aha" experience; and insight is the first step toward constructive change.

Leaders and their subordinates are like partners at a dance. The experience can be very exhilarating, but the dancers can also fall over each other's feet. Both parties carry a heavy responsibility for making the interchange work. Willingness to listen is needed, and respect for other people's point of view is required. Thus, a relationship of trust, making for frank dialogue between leaders and followers, is a precondition for success in preventing regressive behavior in leadership. This necessitates an ability to cope with the outside world in a flexible manner. As we have seen, some leaders are unable to do this. Their behavior seems to be restricted and rigid and they tend to get stuck in vicious circles. Instead of welcoming change and new opportunities, they may react to the outside world in a pathological way.

Paradoxically enough, occasionally it may be exactly this irrational quality that is needed to make a leader effective. Paranoid reactions and visionary experiences may feed very well into certain types of situations; one-sided behavior and overreaction may be exactly what is needed. And many political and religious leaders have acted just this way. We only have to think of leaders such as Joan of Arc or Stalin. However, in spite of the appropriateness of this behavior in some situations, we should not forget its dark side. To evoke regressive tendencies in others and provoke aggression is like being the sorcerer's apprentice. What is set into motion may be impossible to stop.

Leaders are symbols. They are outlets of identification for their followers and serve as scapegoats when things go wrong. In this interactive process, power becomes the binding force between leaders and followers, the currency on which most of these relationships depend. Unfortunately, effective leadership and the wise exercise of power do not necessarily go together. As I have cautioned repeatedly, in the leader-follower dialogue the F-dimension is ever present and may lead to the abuse of power and eventually to the leader's fall. The true leader, however, is the one who knows how to balance reflection and action by using self-insight as a restraining force when the sirens of power are beckoning. In that context Martin Buber's words seem to be very appropriate: "The great man is powerful, involuntarily and composedly powerful, but he is not avid for power. What he is avid for is the realization of what he has in mind, the incarnation of the spirit. So long as a man's power is bound to the goal, the work, the calling, it is, in itself, neither good nor evil, only a suitable or unsuitable instrument. But as soon as this bond with the goal is broken off or loosened, and the man ceases to think of power as the capacity to do something, but thinks of it as a possession, then his power, being cut off and self-satisfied, is evil and corrupts the history of the world."

Chapter Notes

Page   *Chapter 1: The Internal Psychic Theater of the Leader*

4   To use his own words:
        Newsweek, December 24, 1984, 36.

7   Studies of leadership:
        Bernard B. Bass, *Stogdill's Handbook of Leadership* (New
        York: Free Press, 1981).

7   This had caused:
        Aaron Wildavsky, *New York Times Book Review*, April 27,
        1980, 12.

7   These scholars put forth:
        M. T. Hannan and J. H. Freeman, "The Population Ecology
        of Organizations," *American Journal of Sociology* 82 (1977):
        929–64; and Howard E. Aldrich, *Organizations and En-
        vironment* (Englewood Cliffs, NJ: Prentice-Hall, 1979).

7   This "population ecology":
        Jeffrey Pfeffer and Gerald R. Salancik, *The External Con-
        trol of Organizations: A Resource Dependency Perspective*
        (New York: Harper & Row, 1984).

8   To use the words:
        Herbert A. Simon, *Administrative Behavior*, rev. ed. (New
        York: Free Press, 1967), 134.

Page

8   In sharp contrast:
H. Igor Ansoff, *Corporate Strategy* (New York: McGraw-Hill, 1965); Kenneth R. Andrews, *The Concept of Corporate Strategy*, rev. ed. (Homewood, IL: Richard Irwin, 1981); and John Child, "Organization Structure, Environment and Performance: The Role of Strategic Choice," *Sociology* 6 (1972): 2–21.

8   Unfortunately, even if:
Cecil A. Gibb, "Leadership," in G. Lindzey and E. Aronson, *The Handbook of Social Psychology*, vol. 4 (Reading, MA: Addison-Wesley, 1969); Jeffrey Pfeffer, "The Ambiguity of Leadership," *Academy of Management Review* 2 (1977): 104–11; Robert J. House and Mary L. Baetz, "Leadership: Some Empirical Generalizations and New Research Directions," *Research in Organizational Behavior* 1 (1979): 341–423; Bass, *Stogdill's Handbook of Leadership*; and Arthur A. Jago, "Leadership: Perspectives in Theory and Research," *Management Science* 28 (1982): 315–36.

8   This book is different:
Clifford Geertz, *The Interpretation of Culture* (New York: Basic Books, 1973); Clifford Geertz, *Local Knowledge* (New York: Basic Books, 1983); George Devereux, *De L'angoisse à la Methode dans les Sciences du Comportement* (Paris: Flammarion: Nouvelle Bibliothèque Scientifique, 1980); and Manfred F. R. Kets de Vries and Danny Miller, "Interpreting Organizational Text," *Journal of Management Studies* 24 (1987): 233–47.

Chapter 2: Uncovering the Operational Code: The Enigma of Leadership

13   Historians, political and social scientists:
Edward Shils, "Charisma," *International Encyclopedia of the Social Sciences*, vol. 2 (New York: MacMillan and the Free Press, 1968); Robert Tucker, "The Theory of Charismatic Leadership," *Daedalus* 97 (1968); and Ann Ruth

Page

Willner, *The Spellbinders* (New Haven: Yale University Press, 1984).

13   The term *charisma:*
Max Weber, *The Theory of Social and Economic Organization,* trans. A. M. Henderson and Talcott Parsons (New York: Oxford University Press, 1947), 358–59.

14   Weber also mentioned:
Ibid., 363.

15   Ibid.

16   According to the psychoanalyst:
Erik H. Erikson, *Young Man Luther* (New York: W. W. Norton, 1958); and Erik H. Erikson, *Gandhi's Truth: On the Origins of Militant Nonviolence* (New York: W. W. Norton, 1969).

16   It is usually hard:
Nathan Leites, *A Study of Bolshevism* (Glencoe, IL: Free Press, 1953); Alexander L. George, "The Operational Code: A Neglected Approach to the Study of Political Leaders and Decision Making," *International Studies Quarterly* 13 (1969): 190–222; James David Barber, "Strategies for Understanding Politicians," *American Journal of Political Science* (Spring 1974): 443–67; Lester Luborsky, *Principles of Psychoanalytic Psychotherapy* (New York: Basic Books, 1984); and Lester Luborsky, Paul Cristoph, and James Mellon, "Advent of Objective Measures of Transference Concept," *Journal of Consulting and Clinical Psychology* 54 (1986): 39–47.

17   "That's about the best information":
Anne Jardim, *The First Henry Ford: A Study in Personality and Business Leadership* (Cambridge, MA: MIT Press, 1970), 185.

19   His business empire:
Manfred F. R. Kets de Vries and Robert Dick, "Virgin and Richard Branson" (INSEAD case study, 1988).

Page
20 The extent to which private crises:
Harold D. Lasswell, *Psychopathology and Politics* (Chicago: University of Chicago Press, 1930).

21 The Mary Kay Cosmetics:
Roul Tunley, "Mary Kay's Sweet Smell of Success," *Reader's Digest,* November 1978, 112.

22 Jerzy Kosinski, in his novel:
Jerzy Kosinski, *Being There* (New York: Bantam, 1972).

24 Freud, probably influenced:
Sigmund Freud, "Group Psychology and the Analysis of the Ego," *The Standard Edition of the Complete Psychological Works of Sigmund Freud,* vol. 18 (London: Hogarth Press and the Institute of Psychoanalysis, 1921), 70.

26 "We know that in the mass":
Sigmund Freud, "Moses and Monotheism," *Standard Edition,* vol. 23 (1939), 109–10.

Chapter 3: The Mysterious Transformation: Leaders Who Can't Manage
34 What happens:
Josef Breuer and Sigmund Freud, "Studies on Hysteria," *Standard Edition,* vol. 2 (1893–95).

35 This tendency to modify:
Ralph R. Greenson, *The Technique and Practice of Psychoanalysis,* vol. 1 (New York: International Universities Press, 1967); Robert Langs, *The Therapeutic Interaction,* 2 vols. (New York: Jason Aronson, 1976); and Manfred F. R. Kets de Vries and Danny Miller, *The Neurotic Organization: Diagnosing and Changing Counterproductive Styles of Management* (San Francisco: Jossey-Bass, 1984).

35 One common manifestation:
Heinz Kohut, *The Analysis of the Self* (New York: International Universities Press, 1971); and Heinz Kohut and Ernest S. Wolf, "The Disorders of the Self and Their Treatment: An Outline," *International Journal of Psychoanalysis* 59 (1978): 413–26.

Page
38 Like children, such people recognize no middle:
Melanie Klein, *Contributions to Psychoanalysis, 1921–45*
(London: Hogarth Press, 1948); Otto Kernberg, *Object Relations Theory and Clinical Psychoanalysis* (New York: Jason
Aronson, 1976); Otto Kernberg, *Internal World and External Reality* (New York: Jason Aronson, 1985); and Margaret
S. Mahler, Fred Pine, and Anni Bergman, *The Psychological
Birth of the Human Infant* (New York: Basic Books, 1975).

42 An investigation revealed:
Larry Gurwin, "Death of a Banker," *Institutional Investor,*
October 1982, 105–27; and Rupert Cornwell, *God's Banker:
An Account of the Life and Death of Roberto Calvi* (London: Victor Gollancz, 1985).

46 Attachment needs:
John Bowlby, *Attachment and Loss*, vol. 1, *Attachment*
(New York: Basic Books, 1969); and H. F. Harlow and M. K.
Harlow, "The Affectional Systems," in *Behavior in Nonhuman Primates*, vol. 2, ed. A. M. Schrier, H. F. Harlow,
and F. Stollnitz (New York and London: Academic Press,
1965).

47 In fact, many years ago:
Sigmund Freud, "Some Character Types Met within Psychoanalytic Work," *Standard Edition*, vol. 14 (1916).

Chapter 4: The Spectrum of Personalities: Leaders and Followers
56 "Each secret-theatre self":
Joyce McDougall, *Theaters of the Mind* (New York: Basic
Books, 1985), 7.

56 The Diagnostic and Statistical Manual of Mental Disorders: American Psychiatric Association, *DSM III-R:
Diagnostic and Statistical Manual of Mental Disorders*, 3rd
ed. rev. (Washington, DC: APA, 1987).

59 They justify anger and vengeful behavior:
Freud, "Some Character Types Met"; Ben Burnsten, *The*

CHAPTER NOTES

Page

Manipulator (New Haven: Yale University Press, 1973); Howard Wishnie, *The Impulsive Personality* (New York: Plenum Press, 1977); Harry Levinson, "The Abrasive Personality," *Harvard Business Review,* May–June 1978, 86–94; Theodore Millon, *Disorders of Personality, DSM III: Axis II* (New York: John Wiley, 1981); and Theodore Millon, "Personality Types and Their Diagnostic Criteria," in *Contemporary Directions in Psychopathology,* ed. Theodore Millon and Gerald L. Klerman (New York: Guilford Press, 1986).

60 During his ninety-nine days:
Neil Sheehan, *The Arnheiter Affair* (New York: Random House, 1971).

62 In their preoccupation:
David Shapiro, *Neurotic Styles* (New York: Basic Books, 1965); Otto Kernberg, *Borderline Conditions and Pathological Narcissism* (New York: Jason Aronson, 1975); and Kernberg, *Object Relations Theory.*

63 A sense of humour:
W. W. Meissner, *The Paranoid Process* (New York: Jason Aronson, 1978).

63 These people are often:
Viktor Tausk, "On the Origin of the Influencing Machine in Schizophrenia," *Psychoanalytic Quarterly* 2 (1933): 519–56.

64 Inability to contain:
Manfred F. R. Kets de Vries, "Crisis Leadership and the Paranoid Potential," *Bulletin of the Menninger Clinic* 41 (1977): 349–65; and Manfred F. R. Kets de Vries, *Organizational Paradoxes: Clinical Approaches to Management* (London: Tavistock, 1980).

67 Somehow their emotions:
Douglas Labier, "Irrational Behavior in Bureaucracy," in

Page

The Irrational Executive: Psychoanalytic Explorations in Management, ed. Manfred F. R. Kets de Vries (New York: International Universities Press, 1984).

67 The main objective becomes:
David Shapiro, *Neurotic Styles* (New York: Basic Books, 1965); Mardi J. Horowitz, ed., *Hysterical Personality* (New York: Jason Aronson, 1977); Alan Krohn, *Hysteria: The Elusive Neurosis*, Psychological Issues, Monograph 45/46 (New York: International Universities Press, 1978); and Anthony Storr, *The Art of Psychotherapy* (New York: Methuen, 1979), 82–92.

68 He had been working:
Manfred F. R. Kets de Vries and Jane Petrie, "Eli Black and United Brands" (INSEAD case study, 1988).

71 They are loners:
W. R. D. Fairbairn, *An Object Relations Theory of Personality* (New York: Basic Books, 1952); Harry Guntrip, *Schizoid Phenomena, Object Relations and the Self* (New York: International Universities Press, 1969); Kernberg, *Borderline Conditions;* Kernberg, *Object Relations Theory;* Storr, *Art of Psychotherapy;* and Kets de Vries, *Organizational Paradoxes.*

71 To the outside world:
Donald W. Winnicott, *Playing and Reality* (New York: Basic Books, 1971).

72 Followers will find it:
Manfred F. R. Kets de Vries and Danny Miller, *Unstable at the Top* (New York: New American Library, 1988).

72 Only occasionally, when another executive:
Richard C. Hodgson, Daniel J. Levinson, and Abraham Zaleznik, *The Executive Role Constellation: An Analysis of Personality and Role Relations in Management* (Boston: Division of Research, Graduate School of Business Administration, Harvard University, 1965).

Page

72   As a rule:
      Kets de Vries, *Organizational Paradoxes.*

73   "Visitors weren't allowed":
      William Manchester, *The Arms of Krupp* (New York: Bantam Books, 1970), 287.

74   Common characteristics of this personality style:
      Karl Abraham, "Contributions to the Theory of the Anal
      Character," in *Selected Papers on Psychoanalysis* (New
      York: Brunner/Mazel, 1921); Otto Fenichel, *The Psychoanalytic Theory of Neurosis* (New York: W. W. Norton,
      1945); and Wilhelm Reich, *Character Analysis* (New York:
      Farrar, Straus & Giroux, 1949).

75   In their meticulousness:
      See Shapiro, *Neurotic Styles,* and Storr, *Art of Psychotherapy.*

78   These people shift rapidly:
      Reich, *Character Analysis*; and Richard Dean Parsons and
      Robert J. Wicks, eds., *Passive-Aggressiveness: Theory and
      Practice* (New York: Brunner/Mazel, 1983).

81   Because of their excessive dependency needs:
      Karen Horney, *Our Inner Conflicts* (New York: W. W. Norton, 1945); Storr, *Art of Psychotherapy*; and Kets de Vries,
      Organizational Paradoxes.

82   The inability of the parent:
      Mahler, Pine, and Bergman, *Psychological Birth of the
      Human Infant.*

82–   "Never I thought":
83   Ernst Pawell, *The Nightmare of Reason: A Life of Franz
      Kafka* (New York: Vintage Books, 1985), 26–27.

84   Here suffering stands central:
      Reich, *Character Analysis.*

84   In deriving pleasure:
      Fenichel, *Psychoanalytic Theory of Neurosis.*

Page

84   In their inner world:
Theodore Millon, "Interactive Guide to the Millon Clinical
Multiaxial Inventory," in *Advances in Psychological Assessment*, ed. Paul McReynolds and Gordon J. Chelune (San
Francisco: Jossey-Bass, 1984).

84   Among these people:
Freud, "Some Character Types Met."

Chapter 5: Personal Glory and Power: Leadership in a Narcissistic Age

91   The situation in Iran:
Friz Stern, "Fink Shrinks," *New York Review of Books*,
December 19, 1985, 48.

91–   "Narcissism appears realistically":
92   Christopher Lasch, *The Culture of Narcissism* (New York:
W. W. Norton, 1978), 50.

92   One group he called:
Freud, "Some Character Types Met."

92   To illustrate this personality type:
Ibid., 314–15.

93   Freud in his study:
Freud, "Group Psychology and the Analysis of the Ego,"
123–24.

93   According to Freud:
Sigmund Freud, "Libidinal Types," *Standard Edition*, vol.
21 (1931), 21.

93–   ". . . rises to positions of prominence":
94   Lasch, *Culture of Narcissism*, 43–44.

97   There is a "gamesmanlike":
Michael Maccoby, *The Gamesman* (New York: Simon &
Schuster, 1976).

98   Researchers of child development:
Donald W. Winnicott, *The Maturational Process and the*

Page

Facilitating Environment (New York: International Universities Press, 1965); and Donald W. Winnicott, *Through Paediatrics to Psychoanalysis* (New York: Basic Books, 1975).

98–
99

These two narcissistic configurations:
Kohut, *Analysis of the Self.*

99

They are composed of:
Klein, *Contributions to Psychoanalysis*; Edith Jacobson, *The Self and the Object World* (New York: International Universities Press, 1964); Guntrip, *Schizoid Phenomena, Object Relations and the Self*; Winnicott, *Through Paediatrics to Psychoanalysis*; Mahler, Pine, and Bergman, *Psychological Birth of the Human Infant*; Kernberg, *Borderline Conditions*; Kernberg, *Object Relations Theory*; Kernberg, *Internal World and External Reality.*

99

In creating this map :
Jay R. Greenberg and Stephen A. Mitchell, *Object Relations in Psychoanalytic Theory* (Cambridge, MA: Harvard University Press, 1983).

101–
102

For example, the latest version of the DSM III-R:
DSM III-R, 351.

104

In describing messianic and charismatic:
Heinz Kohut, "Creativeness, Charisma, Group Psychology," in *The Search for the Self*, vol. 2, ed. Paul H. Ornstein (New York: International Universities Press, 1978); and Vamik D. Volcan, "Narcissistic Personality Organization and Reparative Leadership," *International Journal of Group Psychotherapy* 30 (1980): 131–52.

105

They couldn't care less:
Kohut and Wolf, "The Disorders of the Self and Their Treatment."

106

Perhaps Freud had this in mind:
Sigmund Freud, "A Childhood Recollection from Dichtung und Wahrheit," *Standard Edition*, vol. 17 (1917), 156.

Page

107   Their leadership style has more of a:
James MacGregor Burns, *Leadership* (New York: Harper & Row, 1978).

108   Independence of thought:
Alice Miller, *Prisoners of Childhood* (New York: Basic Books, 1981), 33–34.

109   Their behavior has an "as if":
Helene Deutsch, *Neuroses and Character Types* (New York: International Universities Press, 1965).

Chapter 6: Folie à Deux: Leaders Driving Their Followers Mad

117   Hoover struck many:
Joseph l. Schott, *No Left Turns* (New York: Praeger, 1975); Manfred F. R. Kets de Vries, "J. Edgar Hoover and the FBI," (INSEAD case study, 1988); Neil J. Welch and David W. Marston, *Inside Hoover's FBI: The Top Field Chief Reports* (Garden City, NY: Doubleday, 1984); and Richard Gid Powers, *Secrecy and Power, The Life of J. Edgar Hoover* (New York: Free Press, 1987).

119– In psychoanalytic and psychiatric literature:
120   Harold F. Searles, *Collected Papers on Schizophrenia and Related Subjects* (New York: International Universities Press, 1965).

120   Two French psychiatrists:
C. Lasèque and J. Fabret, "La Folie à Deux ou Folie Communiquè," *Ann. Med. Psychologie* 5 serie (1877): T. 18.

120   Other names given to this phenomenon:
Helene Deutsch, "Folie à Deux," *Psychoanalytic Quarterly* 7 (1938): 307–18; A. Gralnick, "Folie à Deux—The Psychosis of Association: Review of 103 Cases and Entire English Literature with Presentations," parts 1 and 2, *Psychoanalytic Quarterly* 16 (1942): 230–63, 491–520; Sydney E. Pulver and Manly Y. Brunt, "Deflection of Hostility in

233

Page

Folie à Deux," *Archives of General Psychiatry* 5 (1961): 65–73; and Berchmans Rioux, "A Review of Folie à Deux; The Psychosis of Association," *Psychoanalytic Quarterly* 37 (1963): 405–28.

124   In many instances, the subordinates:
Anna Freud, *The Ego and the Mechanisms of Defense*, rev. ed. (New York: International Universities Press, 1936); and Kets de Vries, *Organizational Paradoxes*.

125   To come back to our example:
Jardim, *The First Henry Ford*.

Chapter 7: The Dark Side of Entrepreneurship
142   Creative entrepreneurs possess:
Manfred F. R. Kets de Vries, "The Entrepreneurial Personality: A Person at the Crossroads," *Journal of Management Studies* 14 (1977): 34–57.

143   "The entrepreneur who starts":
F. Derek du Toit, "Confessions of a Successful Entrepreneur," *Harvard Business Review*, November-December 1980, 44.

144   They come in all shapes:
Norman R. Smith, *The Entrepreneur and His Firm: The Relationship between Type of Man and Type of Company* (East Lansing, MI: Michigan State University, 1967); Herbert A. Wainer and Irwin M. Rubin, "Motivation of Research and Development Entrepreneurs: Determinants of Company Success," *Journal of Applied Psychology* 53 (1969): 178–84; Orvis F. Collins and David G. Moore, *The Organization Makers: A Study of Independent Entrepreneurs* (New York: Meredith, 1970); and John A. Hornaday, "Research about Living Entrepreneurs," in *Encyclopedia of Entrepreneurship*, ed. Calvin A. Kent, Donald L. Sexton, and Karl H. Vesper (Englewood Cliffs, N.J.: Prentice-Hall, 1982).

Page
144   This attitude contrasts:
William E. Henry, "The Business Executive: The Psychodynamics of a Social Role," *American Journal of Sociology* 54 (1949): 286–91.

Chapter 8: The Succession Game
165   Succession at the top:
Oscar Grusky, "Administrative Succession in Formal Organizations," *Social Forces* 39 (1960): 105–15.

168   It has significant effects:
Financial World, "The CEO Factor," December 1981, 21–23.

169   In the light of these psychological forces:
Harry Levinson, "Don't Choose Your Own Successor," *Harvard Business Review*, November–December 1974, 88–97.

170   In spite of the forces of reality:
Elliot Jaques, "Death and the Mid-Life Crisis," *International Journal of Psychoanalysis* 46 (1965): 502–14; Robert Jay Lifton, *Death in Life* (New York: Random House, 1967); and Ernest Becker, *The Denial of Death* (New York: Free Press, 1973).

170   "It is indeed impossible":
Sigmund Freud, "Thoughts for the Times on War and Death," *Standard Edition*, vol. 14 (1915), 289.

171– One obvious way of coping:
172   C. Roland Christensen, *Management Succession in Small and Growing Enterprises* (Boston: Harvard University, Graduate School of Business Administration, Division of Research, 1953); Abraham Zaleznik, *Human Dilemmas of Leadership* (New York: Harper & Row, 1966); and Harry Levinson, *Executive* (Cambridge, MA: Harvard University Press, 1981).

Page
173   The precondition for the successful:
      Freud, "Group Psychology and the Analysis of the Ego";
      Wilfred R. Bion, *Experiences in Groups* (London: Tavistock,
      1959); Irving L. Janis, "Group Identification under Condi-
      tions of External Danger," *British Journal of Medical
      Psychology* 36 (1963): 227–38; and Philip E. Slater,
      Microcosm (New York: Wiley, 1966).

175   The economics of power:
      Michel Crozier, *The Bureaucratic Phenomenon* (Chicago:
      University of Chicago Press, 1964); Mauk Mulder, "Power
      Equalization through Participation," *Administrative
      Science Quarterly* 16 (1971): 31–38; Andrew M. Pettigrew,
      "Toward a Political Theory of Organizational Inter-
      vention," *Human Relations* 28 (1975): 191–208; and Abraham
      Zaleznik and Manfred F. R. Kets de Vries, *Power and the
      Corporate Mind*, rev. ed. (Chicago, IL: Bonus Books, 1985).

177   Unfortunately, research on succession:
      Richard O. Carlson, *Executive Succession and Organiza-
      tional Change* (Danville, IL: Interstate Printers and Pub-
      lisher's 1962); Donald L. Helmich and Warren B. Brown,
      "Succession Type and Organizational Change in the Cor-
      porate Enterprise," *Administrative Science Quarterly*
      17 (1972): 371–81; Donald L. Helmich, "Organizational
      Growth and Succession Patterns," *Academy of Manage-
      ment Journal* 17 (1974): 771–75; Donald L. Helmich, "Cor-
      porate Succession: An Examination," *Academy of Manage-
      ment Journal* 18 (1975): 429–41; Donald L. Helmich, "Suc-
      cession: A Longitudinal Look," *Journal of Business Re-
      search* 4 (1976): 355–64; Gil E. Gordon and Ned Rosen,
      "Critical Factors in Leadership Succession," *Organiza-
      tional Behavior and Human Performance* 27 (1981): 227–
      54; Dan R. Dalton and Idalene F. Kesner, "Inside/Outside
      Succession and Organizational Size: The Pragmatics of
      Executive Replacement," *Academy of Management Jour-*

Page

nal 26 (1983: 736–42; and Kenneth B. Schwarz and Krishnagopal Menon, "Executive Succession in Failing Firms," *Academy of Management Journal* 28 (1985): 680–86.

182   Pleasant memories often function:
Anna Freud, *Ego and the Mechanism of Defense*; Fenichel, *Psychoanalytic Theory of Neurosis*; Charles Brenner, *An Elementary Textbook of Psychoanalysis* (New York: International Universities Press, 1955); and John C. Nemiah, "The Dynamic Bases of Psychopathology," in *The Harvard Guide to Modern Psychiatry*, ed. Armand M. Nicholi (Cambridge, MA: Belknap Press, 1978).

182   Industrial sociologist:
Alvin Gouldner, "The Problem of Succession in Bureaucracy," in *Reader in Bureaucracy*, ed. Robert Merton (Glencoe, IL: Free Press, 1952), 339–51; and Alvin Gouldner, *Patterns of Industrial Bureaucracy* (New York: Free Press, 1954).

183   "the 'dependency' group":
Kernberg, *Internal World and External Reality*, 213.

183   The positive side of this psychological:
Gordon and Rosen, "Critical Factors in Leadership Succession."

183   Given this process:
Edwin Hollander and James Julian, "Studies in Leader Legitimacy, Influence and Innovation and a Further Look at Leader Legitimacy, Influence and Innovation," in *Group Processes*, ed. L. Berkowitz (New York: Academic Press, 1978).

Chapter 9: "I'd Follow That Man—Anywhere—Blindfolded": Effective Leadership

189   As one of his officers:
William Manchester, *American Caesar* (Boston: Little, Brown, 1978), 5.

Page

190   As my discussion:
Erik H. Erikson, *Life History and the Historical Moment*
(New York: W. W. Norton, 1978).

190   In taking this approach:
Bass, *Stogdill's Handbook of Leadership*; Warren Bennis
and Burt Nanus, *Leaders: The Strategy for Taking Charge*
(New York: Harper & Row, 1985); and Harold J. Leavitt,
Corporate Pathfinders (Homewood, IL: Dow Jones–Irwin,
1986).

190   Clearly, one cannot understand:
Abraham Zaleznik, "Managers and Leaders: Are They Different?" *Harvard Business Review*, May–June 1977, 55, 67–
78; Harry Levinson, "Criteria for Choosing Chief Executives," *Harvard Business Review*, July-August 1980, 113–20;
and Kets de Vries and Miller, *The Neurotic Organization*.

190–   "... there can be no prestige":
191   Charles de Gaulle, *The Edge of the Sword* (Westport, CT:
Greenwood Press, 1975), 58–59.

191   In the same vein:
Ibid., 46

191   He adds that the leader:
Ibid., 64.

191   And he continues by saying:
Ibid., 80.

191   He adds that the leader "must outbid":
Ibid, 104.

191   He was one of those leaders:
Burns, *Leadership*.

193   Moreover, these people seem to differ:
Kets de Vries and Danny Miller, *The Neurotic Organiza-
tion*; Zaleznik and Kets de Vries, *Power and the Corporate
Mind*.

Page

193   Hence, these inner scenarios:
        Robert C. Tucker, *Politics as Leadership* (Columbia, MO:
        University of Missouri Press, 1981), 143.

193–   His life's task became:
194   Douglas MacArthur, *Reminiscences* (New York: Da Capo
        Press, 1964), 9.

194   Such exalted imagery:
        Ibid., 18.

194   Again, in his case:
        Leonard Mosley, *Disney's World* (New York: Stein & Day,
        1985).

196   Indeed, Freud compared:
        Freud, "Group Psychology and the Analysis of the Ego," 81.

197   "A group is extraordinarily credulous":
        Ibid., 78.

198   "Mr. Watson is the man":
        Robert Sobel, *IBM: Colossus in Transition* (New York:
        Bantam Books, 1981), 57.

199   As the management theorists:
        W. Morgan McCall, Jr. and Michael M. Lombardo, "What
        Makes a Top Executive?" *Psychology Today*, February
        1983, 28.

200   Effective leaders are also masters:
        Henry Minzberg, *The Nature of Managerial Work* (New
        York: Harper & Row, 1973); John P. Kotter, *The General
        Managers* (New York: Free Press, 1982); and Fred Luthans,
        Stuart A. Rosenkrantz and Harry W. Hennessey, "What
        Do Successful Managers Really Do? An Observation
        Study of Managerial Activities," *Journal of Applied Be-
        havioral Sciences* 21 (1985): 255–70.

200   "Not only did he keep":
        Richard Neustadt, *Presidential Power* (New York: Wiley,
        1960), 157–58.

Page

200   One of the master network builders:
Alfred P. Sloan, *My Years with General Motors* (New York: Doubleday, 1963).

201   Studies of effective leaders:
Daniel J. Isenberg, "How Senior Managers Think," *Harvard Business Review*, November–December 1984, 81–90.

201   They are what has been called:
Z. J. Lipowski, "Sensory and Information Inputs Overload: Behavioral Effects," *Comprehensive Psychiatry* 16 (1975): 199–221.

202   This characteristic enables them:
A. Petrie, *Individuality in Pain and Suffering* (Chicago: University of Chicago Press, 1967).

202   They are flexible:
Peter Suedfeld and A. Dennis Rank, "Revolutionary Leaders: Long-term Success as a Function of Changes in Conceptual Complexity," *Journal of Personality and Social Psychology* 34 (1976): 169–78.

203   Harold Geneen, the former president:
Kets de Vries and Miller, *Unstable at the Top.*

203   Indeed, effective leaders:
Robert J. House, "A 1976 Theory of Charismatic Leadership," in *Leadership: The Cutting Edge*, ed. James G. Hunt and Lars L. Larson (Carbondale, IL: Southern Illinois University Press, 1977).

204–   "West's never unprepared":
205   Tracy Kidder, *The Soul of a New Machine* (Harmondsworth: Penguin Books, 1982), 47.

205   Technical skills are listed:
Bass, *Stogdill's Handbook of Leadership.*

205   Chairman Iacocca of the Chrysler Corporation:
Lee Iacocca, *Iacocca: An Autobiography* (New York: Bantam Books, 1984).

Page
206 They firmly believe:
Julian B. Rotter, "Generalized Expectancies for Internal versus External Control of Reinforcement," *Psychological Monographs* 80 (1966), whole no. 609.

206 In their behavior:
Suzanne R. Kobasa, "Stress Life Events, Personality and Health: An Inquiry into Hardiness," *Journal of Personality and Social Psychology* 37 (1979): 1–11.

207 "I am not an optimist":
Jean Monnet, *Mémoires* (Paris: Fayard, 1976), 44.

207 Although Walt Disney:
Mosley, *Disney's World.*

208 They go one step further:
Karl E. Weick, *The Social Psychology of Organizing,* 2nd ed. (Reading, MA: Addison-Wesley, 1979).

208 An excellent case in point:
Akio Morita (with Edwin M. Reingold and Mitsuko Shimomura), *Made in Japan* (New York: Dutton, 1986); and P. Ranganath Nayak and John M. Ketteringham, *Breakthroughs!* (New York: Rawson Associates, 1986).

209 They are willing to take:
David C. McClelland, *The Achieving Society* (Princeton: Van Nostrand, 1961).

Chapter 10: The Leader as Symbol
215 He was in fact a model:
Ken Auletta, *The Art of Corporate Success* (New York: Putnam's, 1984), 31.

216 He said:
Ibid., 62.

216 He would say:
Schlumberger Annual Report, 1985, 4.

Page

217   As he said himself:
        Auletta, *Art of Corporate Success*, 98.

217   He didn't want his people:
        Annual Report, 4.

217   He said:
        Auletta, *Art of Corporate Success*, 115.

217   As we can see from the case:
        Donald A. Schön, *The Reflective Practitioner* (New York:
        Basic Books, 1983).

219   Also, organizational processes:
        Graham Allison, *Essence of Decision: Explaining the
        Cuban Missile Crisis* (Boston: Little, Brown, 1971).

219   Social systems have their own way:
        Elliot Jaques, "Social Systems as Defense against
        Persecutory and Depressive Anxiety," in *New Directions
        in Psychoanalysis*, ed. J. Rivière (New York: Jason Aron-
        son, 1956); Isabel E. P. Menzies, "A Case Study in the Func-
        tioning of Social Systems as a Defense against Anxiety,"
        Human Relations 13 (1960): 95–121; and Kets de Vries and
        Miller, *Unstable at the Top*.

Index

Acton, Lord, 32
American Caesar, 189
American Psychiatric Association, 56
American Seal-Cap Corporation, 68
Arctos, Inc., 34
Arms of Krupp, 73
Arnheiter, Marcus, A., 60–61, 64
AT&T breakup, 4
Ataturk, Kemal, 14

Baedeker Corporation, 57
BANCO Ambrosiano, 42
Bank failures
  Franklin National Bank, 7
  Penn Square Bank, 7
Bank of Italy, 42
Being There, 22
Ben-Gurion, David, 14
Bennett, Harry, 25, 26, 125
Black, Eli, 68–69, 71
Boesky, Ivan, 24
Bohlton Company, 165–168, 177
Bonaparte, Napoleon, 14, 204
Branson, Richard, 19–20, 21, 109,
  189
Branson, Sir George, 20
Buber, Martin, 221
Business failures
  DeLorean Motors, 6
  Guinness, 6
  Investment Overseas Services, 6

Caine Mutiny, 60
Caligula, Emperor of Rome, 33
Calvi, Roberto, 42–43, 46, 47
Carlzon, Jan, 14
Castro, Fidel, 14
CBS, 176
Charisma, 9, 13–16, 22, 23, 34, 111,
  122, *see also* Leadership,
  charismatic
  definition, 13–15
Chrysler Corporation, 5, 14, 205
Churchill, Winston, 197

Clair, Lise, 34–35
Clark, Robert, 31–32, 41
Collective Insanity, *see* Folie à deux
Concorde Corporation, 180
Core conflictual relationship themes,
  16–21, 23, 56, 210
  definition, 16
Cornfeld, Bernard, 6
Culture of Narcissism, The, 91

Dalton Corporation, 49
Data General Corporation, 204
De Benedetti, Carlo, 3–5, 109, 189
De Gaulle, Charles, 190–191, 203,
  204, 205
DeLorean Motors, 6
DeLorean, John, 6
Delusional behavior, *see* Folie à deux
Dependency, *see* Disposition
*Diagnostic and Statistical Manual of
  Mental Disorders (DSM III-R)*,
  56, 57, 70, 101–102
Dionysius, tyrant of Syracuse, iv
Disney Corporation, 207
Disney, Roy, 207
Disney, Walt, 194–195, 207–208
Disneyland, 208
Disposition
  aggressive, 57–60
  controlling, 72–76, 82, 87, 125, 144,
    145, 146, 147,
  dependent, 51, 66, 79–82, 83, 84,
    88, 112, 119, 121, 122, 123, 124,
    154, 196
  detached, 68–72, 79, 82, 86, 87
    avoidant, 70, 71
    schizoid, 70
  histrionic, 64–67, 79, 82, 88
  hybrids, 85–88
  masochistic, 82–85, 88
  narcissistic, 36, 51, 56, 67, 87, 88,
    91–113, 131, 150, 151
    constructive, 108–109, 110, 112,
      193

Disposition, narcissistic, *continued*
  definition, 101–102
  reactive, 104–105, 107, 108, 109
  self-deceptive, 105–108, 109
  paranoid, 39, 41, 60–64, 75, 79, 86,
    87, 119, 120, 121, 125, 131, 217,
    220
  passive-aggressive, 76–79
Du Toit, F. Derek, 143
DuMaurier, Daphne, 182

Electronic Data Systems (EDS), 5, 6
Entrepreneurs
  applause desire, 149–151
  as subordinates, 143, 145, 146, 148,
    152, 157, 158, 159
  characteristics, 142–144
  defensive patterns, 151–154, 155,
    156
Entrepreneurship, 9, 139–161
  control, 144–147
  distrust, 147–149
  outside influence, 160
Erikson, Erik, 16

F-dimension (failure factor), viii, 7,
  9, 10, 15, 17, 24, 26, 27, 33, 37,
  39, 41, 42, 44, 47, 52, 55, 87, 111,
  125, 136, 143, 156, 169, 176, 186,
  190, 210, 218, 221
Failure factor, *see* F-dimension
Fantasia, 208
Federal Bureau of Investigation
  (FBI), 117–118
Fewings, Helene, 85
Fiat, 4
Folie à deux, 120–136, 210
  by entrepreneurs, 154–156
  definition, 120
  detection, 131–133
  scapegoating, 127–130
  solutions, 133–136
Follett, Ken, 6
Ford Motor Company, 25
Ford, Henry, 17–19, 21, 25, 33, 126,
  194
  Oslo peace ship, 17
Ford, Henry, II, 26
Forester, C. S., 61
Fortune magazine, 4, 57
Franklin National Bank, 7

Freud, Sigmund, 24, 26, 47, 92, 93,
  106, 108, 170, 196, 197
Fulton, Larry, 49

Gadhafi, Moammar, 33, 91
Gandhi, Mahatma, 16, 192
Gaylin, Willard, 55
Geneen, Harold, 203
General Motors Corporation, 126,
  200–201
Gouldner, Alvin, 182
Grace, Peter, 176
Grace, W. R., Corporation, 176
Great Depression, 192
Guinness, 6

Hammer, Armand, 5, 176
Harris, Peter, 44–46
Harvard Business School, viii
Harvey-Jones, John, 14
Hitler, Adolph, 24, 33, 91, 105, 118,
  192, 197
  and Final Solution, 24
Homo politicus, 20
Honda Motor Company, 5
Honda, Soichiro, 5
Hoover, J. Edgar, 117–119
Hornblower, Horatio, 61
Howell, Ted, 39–41
Hughes, Howard, 33, 71

Iacocca, Lee, 5, 14, 205–206
IBM Corporation, 198–199
  Hundred Percent Club, 199
ICI, 14
Idealization, 35–37, 99, 104, 108, 113,
  122, 184, 196
Investment Overseas Services, 6
Iran, 91
Iran–Contra arms deal, 127
Isolation, 44–47, 74
Israel effect, 4
Italy
  economic turnaround, 4
  industrial malaise, 4
ITT Corporation, 203

Jefferson, Thomas, 10
Joan of Arc, 220
Jones, Rev. Jim, 24, 118
Jonestown massacre, 24

Kafka, Franz, 83
  Letter to His Father, 83
Kay, Mary, 21, *see also* Mary Kay
  Cosmetics
Kennedy, John F., 109, 197, 203
Kent, Howard, 34–35
Kernberg, Otto, 183
Khomeini, Ayatollah, 91
Kidder, Tracy, 204
King Lear Syndrome, *see*
  Succession
King, Martin Luther, Jr., 192
Kipling, Rudyard, 201
Kohut, Heinz, 104
Kozinski, Jerzy, 22
Kramer, Ted, 80
Krupp von Bohlen und Halbach,
  Gustav, 72–73
Krupp, Alfred, 72
Krupp, Bertha, 72
Krupp, House of, 72–73

Lang, Tom, 180
Larix Corporation, 39–41
Lasch, Christopher, 91–92, 93
Lasswell, Harold, 20
Lawrence, Peter, 175–176
Le Bon, G, 197
Leadership
  charismatic, 13–16, 21, 22, 23, 39,
    91, 93, 191
  effective, 189–190
  characteristics, 190–191, 211
    competence, 205–206, 209, 210
    empowerment, 203–205
    enactment, 208–209
    hardiness, 206–208, 209, 210
    managing meaning, 195–199
    network building, 199–201, 209
    pattern recognition, 201–203
    perseverance, 206–208, 209,
      210
    reflection, 217, 218
    vision, 16, 46, 192–195, 209
  failures, 6
    Bernard Cornfeld, 6
    Ernest Saunders, 6
    John DeLorean, 6
  messianic, 91, 93
  safeguards, 219–220

Lehman Brothers, 68
Lenin, V. I., 14
Levinson, Harry, 169
Libya, 91
Liebold, E. G., 25, 125
Lombardo, Michael M., 199
Lotar, 76
Lowell, Norman, 57–58
Ludwig, King of Bavaria, 33
Luther, Martin, 16

MacArthur, Douglas, 189, 193–194,
  197
  Reminiscences, 193
Malcolm, Larry, 145–146
Manchester, William, 73, 189
Mao Tse-tung, 14
Marionette theory, 7, 8
Mary Kay Cosmetics, 21, 197
McCall, W. Morgan, 199
McDougall, Joyce, 56
McLuhan, Marshall, 21
Medex Corporation, 79
Mein Kampf, 192
Mental contagion, *see* Folie à deux
Milton, Lester, 139–142
Mirror transference, *see*
  Transference
Monnet, Jean, 207
Morita, Akio, 208
Munro, Jim, 94–97, 101, 105, 113
Murphy, Anne, 64–66
Mussolini, Benito, 105

Narcissism, *see* Disposition
Nasser, Gamal Abdul, 14
National Cash Register, 198
Nehru, Jawaharlal, 109
Neilson, Lawrence, 76–77
Nelson, Lord, 61
Neustadt, Richard, 200
New Deal, 192
Nixon, Richard M., 48–49, 51
Nkrumah, Kwame, 14
Nolan, Ed, 165–168
Nolan, Ted, 49–51
Noro Corporation, 44–46

Occidental Petroleum, 5, 176
Olivetti Corporation, 3–4
On Wings of Eagles, 6

Paley, William, 176
Paranoia, see Disposition, and see
  Entrepreneurship, distrust
Participatative management, 32
Patterson, John, 198
Penn Square Bank, 7
Perfectionism, 74
Perot, H. Ross, 5–6
Pine, Fred, 175–176
Plato, iii, iv
  Academy, iv
  Republic, iii
Population ecology outlook, 7
Post, David, 76–77
Projection, 22–27, 34, 62, 63, 108,
  153, 173, 193, 197
Psychopathology and Politics, 20
Psychosis of association, see Folie à
  deux

Queeg, Captain, 60

Reaction formation, 74
Rebecca myth, see Succession
Reed, Bob, 165–168
Riboud, Jean, 215–218
Richard III, 92
Roosevelt, Franklin D., 14, 192, 197,
  200

Salar Corporation, 139–142
SAS, 14
Saul, King of Israel, 33
Saunders, Ernest, 6
Scapegoating, 47, 153, 184, 196, see
  also Folie à deux
Schlumberger, 215–216
Shakespeare, William, 92, 174, 182
Shared madness, see Folie à deux
Simmons, Chris, 79–80
Simon, Herbert, 8
Sindona, Michele, 43
Sloan, Alfred P., 200–201
Snow White, 207
Solan Corporation, 31–32
Sony Corporation, 208
Sorenson, C. E., 25, 125
Splitting, 62, 108, 151, 196
  definition, 151

Stalin, Josef, 105, 220
Star, Karen, 139–142
Stodgill's Handbook of Leadership,
  205
Strategic choice theory, 8
Substance abuse, 47
  alcoholism, 50
Success
  fear of, 47–52
Succession, 9, 165–186
  choosing a successor, 177
    inside/outside choice, 167,
    177–181
  role of the board, 184–186
  transition, 181–184
    Rebecca myth, 182
  unconscious sabotage, 170–177
    avoiding favoritism, 173–174
    denial of death, 170–171
    King Lear syndrome, 174–176
    leaving a legacy, 171–173
Sukarno, 14

Territorialism, 128, 129
Thatcher, Margaret, 20
Thoreau, Henry David, 8
"Those Wrecked by Success," 47
Tito, Marshal, 14
Transference, 26, 27, 35, 119, 122,
  123, 196
  definition, 35
  mirror, 36–37, 38, 104

UK 2000 campaign, 20
United Brands, 68, 69
United Fruits Company, 68
USS Vance, 60

Virgin Atlantic, 19
Vision, see Leadership

Watson, Thomas, Sr., 198
Weber, Max, 13, 14, 15
Welles, Orson, iv, v
West, Tom, 204–205
Workmens' Accident Insurance In-
  stitute, 83

Zaleznik, Abraham, iv